Safe in the Arms of God

Other Books by John MacArthur

Safe in the Arms of God

Truth from Heaven About the Death of a Child

John MacArthur

NELSON BOOKS
A Division of Thomas Nelson Publishers
Since 1798

www.thomasnelson.com

Published in Nashville, TN, by Thomas Nelson. Thomas Nelson is a trademark of Thomas Nelson, Inc.

Thomas Nelson, Inc. titles may be purchased in bulk for educational, business,fund-raising, or sales promotional use. For information, please e-mail SpecialMarkets@ThomasNelson.com.

Published in association with the literary agency of Wolgemuth & Associates, Inc.

Scripture quotations are from THE NEW KING JAMES VERSION. Copyright © 1979, 1980, 1982, Thomas Nelson, Inc., Publishers.

Library of Congress Cataloging-in-Publication Data

MacArthur, John, 1939-
    Safe in the arms of God : truth from heaven about the death of a child / John MacArthur.
    p. cm.
    Includes bibliographical references.
    ISBN 10: 0-7852-6343-8
    ISBN 13: 978-0-7852-6343-2
    1. Consolation. 2. Infants (Newborn)—Death—Religious aspects—Christianity. 3. Fetal death—Religious aspects—Christianity. 4. Children—Death—Religious aspects—Christianity. 5. Bereavement—Religious aspects—Christianity. I. Title.
BV4907.M23 2003
248.8'66—dc21

                                            2003006567

Dedicated to the sweet memories of little ones gone to heaven from the families of my flock, some of whose parents share their triumphant testimonies in this book.

Contents

Safe in the Arms of God

ONE

Where Is My Child?

"WHAT ABOUT A TWO-YEAR-OLD BABY CRUSHED AT the bottom of the World Trade Center?"

The question was fired at me by Larry King. I had been invited to participate as a panel member on the *Larry King Live* television program one Saturday evening. The program was taped in the aftermath of the September 11, 2001, attacks on the United States. Even though we had been discussing issues of life and death, grief and hope, as part of this program, Larry's question seemed to come out of nowhere.

"Instant heaven," I immediately replied.

Larry fired back a second question: "He wasn't a sinner?"

I again answered, "Instant heaven."

Larry's compelling questions revealed a nagging, troubling issue in the human heart.

What *is* the future of a baby crushed by the rubble of the collapsing World Trade Center? What about any baby that dies? What happens to an unborn child, an infant, a child, or even a physically mature but mentally handicapped adult with the mental capacity of a child after he dies? What is the fate of that "little one" as he or she enters eternity? The questions are agonizing ones for many parents, Christians and non-Christians alike.

A number of rather strange and ill-founded answers have been given to these questions in the past. The *correct* answer, however, begins very simply: "Instant heaven."

In the sound-bite environment of a program such as *Larry King Live*, I had no opportunity to follow up with an explanation for my statement and, frankly, Larry didn't ask for one. He seemed satisfied with my quick and decisive response and went on to other questions related to the ways in which our nation was grieving and recovering from the aftermath of that terrible day of tragedy.

But I believe you deserve an expanded answer because in all likelihood, you are reading this book after having experienced the loss of a child—or perhaps because you are a person in a position, as I have been too many times as pastor, to counsel or encourage someone who has lost a child. My heart grieves with any parent who loses a child, and that is what motivated me to search Scriptures on this subject so I could reach out and offer biblically founded words of comfort and encouragement.

I also suspect that our *need* for answers to questions about the death of children will continue to grow. As our nation contemplates the role we need to take in confronting natural disasters, hunger, and situations of suffering in faraway places, the question always arises, "What about the children who have died or are facing near-certain death?"

When our nation considers war, the question arises, "What about the innocent children who will die?"

As we contemplate the death of children—many of whom are members of families in cultures that practice false religions or participate in no religion—the question arises in the hearts of many Christians, "What happens to *those* little ones?"

Our concerns related to death always seem more profound and heartrending when we are dealing with the death of a child. An accident or illness seems especially tragic and poignant when the life of a little one is lost.

Millions Are Dying . . . or Are They Living?

The great and sad reality is, throughout history, hundreds of millions, perhaps billions, of unborn babies, newborns, and young children have died. Millions are dying in our era.

In the original creation, Adam and Eve lived without the reality of death. According to Genesis 1:26–28, mankind was given the power to produce life in a deathless world. Adam and Eve were expected to "be fruitful and multiply"—to procreate and fill the earth with children who would never know death. God's original plan was that all lives ever conceived would live for all eternity.

When Adam and Eve sinned, death became a reality. The curse of death on the lives of the original parents became the

3

curse of death on the life of every individual ever conceived. Death became a reality not only for the mature, but for the immature as well. From the first days of history to the present, it is not at all an exaggeration to speculate that half of all persons ever conceived died prior to reaching maturity.

I recently read some fairly startling statistics:

- About 25 percent of all conceptions do not complete the twentieth week of pregnancy. In other words, at least one out of four persons conceived die in the womb. Seventy-five percent of these deaths occur in the first twelve weeks.

- Perinatal death—death at the time of birth—continues to occur in massive numbers around the world, even with the advances of modern medical science. One world health organization reported that 4,350,000 babies died at birth in the year 1999, but many experts believe the actual figure is much higher. They estimate that closer to ten million babies die at birth around the world every year, since most losses aren't reported.

The highest rates of infant mortality, of course, tend to occur in the poorest and most primitive nations, especially in Africa and Asia. These nations are also the most pagan. In Afghanistan, for example, the rate of infant mortality is at least 150 babies out of every 1,000. In Angola, the rate is even higher—200 babies out of every 1,000 die at birth or very shortly thereafter. And then there are the horrific abortion statistics we're all familiar with.

If you begin to add up the millions over the years of history, there are countless billions of persons who have entered eternity prior to reaching maturity.

Where are the souls of these persons? They are either populating hell at an incredible rate, populating heaven at an incredible rate, or perhaps populating both heaven and hell at the same incredible rate. Which is it?

We Need Answers Rooted in Truth

"Is my baby in heaven?"

If someone asked you that question, how would *you* respond?

There are those who answer the question out of sentimentality, or out of what they *hope* is true. If pressed, the only argument they are likely to give is that they don't want to believe God would ever refuse a precious little one. A universalist has a quick answer because he believes *everyone* goes to heaven at death. At the other end of the spectrum are those who believe that an unborn child has no soul and therefore has no eternal fate. In between are those who hold a variety of opinions and beliefs. Some declare that only certain "elect" infants go to heaven, while the "non-elect" suffer endless punishment. Others believe infant baptism inoculates a child against hell and secures a place in heaven, but they leave out the souls of those who die prior to birth. Still others believe that all children who die go to heaven because God sovereignly chooses to extend His special grace to them.

My answer to Larry King may have seemed quick, even glib, to you as you read it. But it was not an off-the-cuff answer. Very early in my ministry, I confronted this question about the destiny of little ones who die. My search for an answer rooted in Scripture began in the aftermath of a crisis on a Saturday morning.

At the time, I had a pastor's study that looked out on a courtyard at our church. The sign on the sliding-glass patio door clearly stated "Pastor's Office." I should not have been surprised, therefore, by what happened that morning as I sat in my study putting the finishing touches on the next morning's sermon.

A woman came to the patio door and pounded on it. I quickly rushed to open the door only to hear her exclaim in great anguish, "Please come! I think my baby has died!"

I hurriedly followed her to a house just a few doors down from the church. And sadly, upon entering her home I found her infant child lying lifeless in his crib.

I heard myself saying to this distraught young mother what I trusted would be words of comfort: "Your baby is in heaven. He is safe in the arms of God."

She wept uncontrollably at first, but then, as those words sank into her spirit, she grew more calm. I stayed with her until emergency workers and close relatives could arrive to be with her, and then I returned to my pastor's study—shaken by the abruptness of the interruption, the finality of that tiny baby's death, and also by what I had said from my pastor's heart.

In the days that followed, I reflected a number of times on the experience. I intuitively felt that I had said the right thing to this bewildered and grieving mother, but I also had a strong compulsion to know with certainty that I had spoken the truth to her. Had I spoken to her what could be supported by God's Word? Or had I spoken to her only what I thought would calm and comfort her in the emotional desperation of that moment?

I began a study of the Scriptures about the death of infants and children—including those who die in the womb, those who die at birth, and those who never fully grow mentally to the point of being capable of discerning right from wrong. And it was out of that study that I reached the conclusions presented in this book. I should warn you that this is by no means a typical, schmaltzy "comfort" book. Because I am convinced that the only true comfort comes from God's Word, I will be addressing topics such as sin, the age of accountability, and predestination. I think you'll be grateful for this approach in the end because you won't need to rely on sentiment or well wishes for peace of mind and heart; you'll be able to rely on God's Word. Emotions come and go, but the truth of God's Word is completely consistent and reliable.

My response to Larry King was not an out-of-the-blue response to an out-of-the-blue question. It was a statement of my true conviction based upon a thorough and careful study of Scripture through the years.

"Instant heaven" truly is the destiny of infants and children. Let me tell you *why* that is true.

TWO

What Can We Say with Certainty to Those with Empty Arms?

LILY AWOKE EARLIER THAN USUAL THAT MORNING, and her first thought was to go to the cradle of her child. She had given birth to baby Eunice three days earlier, and Lily had a great sense of satisfaction at having a daughter to join her two rambunctious sons. From the beginning, however, little Eunice had been listless and pale, unlike her brothers after their births. She seemed to shiver frequently, as if deeply cold on the inside, although Lily and the midwife who attended her could detect no fever. Because of their concern she might be cold, they kept her cradle close to the fire.

Lily's immediate concern as she entered the living room that morning was that the fire had gone out—not even a red glow came from the coals. She immediately rushed to the cradle to lift Eunice from it, feeling an overwhelming maternal instinct to cover her with her own warmth. To her horror, the baby was stiff and lifeless. Sometime between Lily's checking on her baby at one o'clock in the morning and coming to her at five o'clock, Eunice had died.

Lily's mournful wail awoke her husband and sons. She could not be consoled and for hours refused to release Eunice from her arms as she rocked back and forth, sobbing loudly. Finally her husband, Marvin, said to the boys, "We need to let your mother be alone for a while." The three of them stoked the fire in the fireplace, closed the door into the living room, and left Lily to mourn until she had cried all the tears she could cry. She eventually slumped over in a deep sleep, and it was then that Marvin was able to take the baby from her arms and call both the preacher and the local doctor.

A simple graveside service was held in the cold afternoon of the next day. The preacher said a few words as the little casket was lowered into the ground, and the family went home to the silence of a house normally filled with laughter, warmth, and the aroma of Lily's nearly constant cooking of soups and stews.

Word soon circulated through the rural community that Lily had given birth and the baby had lived only three days. The vast majority of friends and neighbors learned of the loss only after Eunice had been buried. Very few ever mentioned the birth of the baby to Marvin or Lily. Only one boy came to their sons at school and said, "I heard about your sister. I'm sorry that happened." Only a handful of their friends and fellow church members came to call on Lily and Marvin at their home.

The wife of one couple that came to call said to Lily, "It was for the best, dear. It's best you forget this ever happened. We don't ever need to talk about it again."

Lily could not imagine how she could ever forget. And why should she never want to talk about her daughter again? Eunice had lived inside her for nine months, if only outside her womb for three days. She was a person and a family member, and Lily believed her baby should be remembered by those who loved her.

Another woman said to her, "It's too bad you let that fire go out."

Lily was shocked that her friends might think she had killed her own daughter through neglect. It hadn't even dawned on her until that moment to consider that her baby had died because she failed to stay awake and keep logs on the fire.

The worst thing Lily heard in the aftermath of her daughter's death, however, was something she *overheard* a woman say to Marvin: "God must not have wanted Lily to have a daughter."

Lily was crushed to the core of her soul. What kind of God would be so cruel as to entrust Lily with a pregnancy, but then think her so unfit as a mother that He would immediately take the child she bore?

In many ways, Lily never recovered from the birth and death of her little girl. There was no explanation for her baby's sickness or death—her birth occurred in the first part of the twentieth century, and no one had yet coined the phrase "sudden infant death syndrome."

Lily—who had once been known throughout the area as a

vivacious, fun-loving, spirited woman—became quiet and withdrawn, perpetually sad. Without the resources and counseling readily available today, Lily remained depressed for several years. One night, without her husband knowing she had left the house, she took a long walk in a snowstorm. The cold she developed turned into pneumonia, and with no sign at all that she had a will to live, Lily died two weeks later—at home, just a few feet away from the empty cradle that still occupied its place before the fireplace.

Lily's story is repeated countless times around the world, every day. Babies are born. Babies fail to thrive. Babies die after a few hours or days.

In some cases, the cause of the death is known—in thousands more cases around the world the cause is never known.

Parents have very intense reactions to the death of a child. These reactions, however, are rarely acknowledged or addressed by the public at large and, as a result, these reactions are often private, intense, and unresolved.

A number of years ago I read an article titled "Mental Reactions to Perinatal Death" that recounted statistics related to parental reactions in the aftermath of a baby's death:

- Sixty percent of the parents felt angry.

- Fifty percent of the fathers and ninety percent of the mothers felt guilt.

- Seventy-five percent were irritable.

- Sixty-five to seventy-five percent of the parents lost their appetite and eighty to ninety percent had difficulty sleeping.

- Ninety-five to one hundred percent of the parents felt a profound and deep sadness.[1]

While many of these statistics may be in line with other statistics related to how a person grieves, the statistics related to guilt and anger are significantly higher.

When you consider that millions of babies die each year, the grief experienced by even more millions of parents creates something of a shadow on the soul of our nation—indeed, upon the soul of the world.

Where is hope for these parents?

What is the answer from God's Word?

Of one thing I am certain. Lily's family, friends, and church community ought to have comforted her with *answers* from the Bible rather than questions about why God allowed the child to die and whether Lily was in any way to blame. She needed to be encouraged and helped out of her depression. Most of all, she needed to be given the truth of God's Word.

You Deserve an Answer from God's Word

Several years ago I was asked to participate on a panel at a large conference. Three other pastors joined me on this question-and-answer panel. One of the questions that came from the audience was, "What happens to babies when they die?" The answer of the other three pastors was, essentially, "I don't know."

I was dismayed. How can a person be a pastor and not have an answer to that question? How can a pastor even offer counsel or encouragement to those who experience the loss of a child unless he has answers to the concerns of a grieving heart?

When my turn came to reply I said, "They go to heaven." I then shared an explanation from the Scripture.

Those who are grieving *deserve* a compassionate answer rooted in the truth of Scripture. The parents need them, family members need them, friends need them, pastors and counselors need them. And as I have learned, scriptural answers without comfort will fall on deaf ears, and comfort without Scripture will never completely heal and uplift a grieving heart.

When we look into the grave of a little one, we must not place our hope or trust in a false promise, in an unbiblical theology, in the instability of sentimentalism, or in the cold analysis of human logic. Rather, we must look to what God's Word has to say on the matter. We are called to be faithful to the Word and place our faith in Christ. We are challenged to claim the promises of the Scriptures and live in the assurance of the grace of our Lord. We need words from heaven on the death of a child.

Our answer from Scripture begins with a very simple but all-important statement: *Every life conceived is a person.*

The Bible is very clear on this point: Life begins at conception. Any death that occurs after the moment of conception is the death of a *person*. And *persons* have eternal souls. Anything else we say must be based on this foundational truth.

Scripture gives us six powerful truths about the *personhood* of every child conceived.

Six Precious Truths About Your Life and Your Baby's Life

One of the most comforting passages in the entire Bible is Psalm 139. David writes eloquently about the way God regards him and every human being:

> How precious also are Your thoughts to me, O God!
> How great is the sum of them!
> If I should count them, they would be more in number than
> the sand. (vv. 17–18)

David greatly values the "thoughts" of God toward his own life. He calls them *precious*. He takes comfort and delight in the fact that God's thoughts toward him are too numerous for him to count.

What are these precious thoughts to which David alludes? David identifies six profound truths in the previous verses of this psalm.

1. God knows everything about you before your conception.

The first statement David makes in Psalm 139 is that the Lord knows *everything* about him. He opens his psalm with these words:

> O LORD, You have searched me and known me.
> You know my sitting down and my rising up;
> You understand my thought afar off.
> You comprehend my path and my lying down,
> And are acquainted with all my ways.
> For there is not a word on my tongue,
> But behold, O LORD, You know it altogether. (vv. 1–4)

David notes that the Lord knows every detail of every moment of his life, even when he stands up and sits down. God knows his thoughts, his comings and goings, his habits and inclinations, and his personality traits. The phrase "not a word on my tongue" means "even before I spoke or was capable of speaking." David says that the Lord knew what he would say even before he opened his mouth to speak, even before he could form words in his mouth.

The same is true for you and me. God is intimately acquainted with every detail of your life, from conception to the moment you enter eternity. He knows *all* you say, do, think, and feel. Indeed, He knew *all* about you even before you had words in your mouth or thoughts in your mind, even before you could walk or act on your own.

The same is true, of course, for your baby. God knows *all* that is in the heart and mind of your child—even before your child has a fully developed body and brain in which to embody and voice thoughts and feelings.

2. God is actively involved in your life. David affirms in Psalm 139 that the Lord has a plan and purpose for every life. He controls the things that happen to us, in us, around us, and through us. David wrote:

> You have hedged me behind and before,
> And laid Your hand upon me.
> Such knowledge is too wonderful for me;
> It is high, I cannot attain it. (vv. 5–6)

Nobody can get away from God's active role in his or her life. The Lord is above, below, and all around. We are firmly and fully within His grasp every moment of our existence. God is completely in control of our lives. So, too, He is in complete control of the life of your little one.

For the vast majority of those who are conceived, avoiding death is very difficult. The forces of death are very strong against the conceived child, even in the womb. Many are miscarried or aborted. In primitive, poor areas of the world, the forces of death are also very strong against a baby at birth and in the months immediately following birth. To live and thrive involves an intense struggle—life is far from an automatic "given."

The successful *birth* of any child is regarded in the Scriptures as an act authorized by God. In the psalms we also find these words of David:

> But You are He who took Me out of the womb;
> You made Me trust while on My mother's breasts.
> I was cast upon You from birth.
> From My mother's womb
> You have been My God. (Ps. 22:9–10)

The decision about whether a baby lives or dies is God's decision. He allows conception. He allows birth. He also allows death at birth. He allows what is in keeping with His purposes. No death or life occurs apart from the purposes of God.

God is actively involved in every feature of every life, including whether a child is *born* or dies in the womb, and whether a child lives *past* birth or dies at birth.

3. God will never cease to have knowledge of you. The Lord will never forget, overlook, or lose sight of anyone. David wrote:

> Where can I go from Your Spirit?
> Or where can I flee from Your presence?
> If I ascend into heaven, You are there;
> If I make my bed in hell, behold, You are there.
> If I take the wings of the morning,
> And dwell in the uttermost parts of the sea,

Even there Your hand shall lead me,
And Your right hand shall hold me. (Ps. 139:7–10)

You cannot go anywhere without the Lord knowing precisely where you are. The same is true for your baby.

4. God is never limited in His understanding. Nothing can ever cause God to have a diminished understanding about your life. Metaphorically speaking, the light can never become so dim that God fails to see you fully. No one can ever fall into any situation or circumstance that is shielded from God's view. David wrote:

If I say, "Surely the darkness shall fall on me,"
Even the night shall be light about me;
Indeed, the darkness shall not hide from You,
But the night shines as the day;
The darkness and the light are both alike to You.
(Ps. 139:11–12)

God knew as much about you in the first few moments after your conception as He knows about you today. He sees you fully and completely in the context of eternity, not time. He sees you in detail as He has made you, and that perspective on your life is not in any way inhibited, impeded, or blocked by any circumstance or experience that might come upon you. The same holds true for your baby.

5. God is your personal Creator. You may think that your parents are responsible for having made you the way you are, but God's Word says otherwise. The Bible declares that God is the Creator of all life. He is the One who knit together the strands of DNA that make up your genetic code. He is the One who built into you all the personality traits, abilities, talents, and spiritual gifts that you have. He is the One who gave you your mother's smile, your father's toes, your grandfather's dimple, or your grandmother's eyes. David wrote so beautifully:

> You formed my inward parts;
> You covered me in my mother's womb.
> I will praise You, for I am fearfully and wonderfully made;
> Marvelous are your works,
> And that my soul knows very well.
> My frame was not hidden from You,
> When I was made in secret,
> And skillfully wrought in the lowest parts of the earth.
> (Ps. 139:13–15)

You may think you "made" your baby. Not so. God made your baby and breathed life into him or her. Your child is *His* creation.

6. God personally planned your destiny. God numbered your days and authorized His special purpose for them. David wrote:

Your eyes saw my substance, being yet unformed.
And in Your book they all were written,
The days fashioned for me,
When as yet there were none of them. (Ps. 139:16)

The same is true for your child. God knew precisely how long your child would live and for what purpose your child would live. Your child's destiny was and is in His hands.

The word of the Lord came to the prophet Jeremiah in a way very similar to that experienced by David. In the opening passage of Jeremiah's prophecy we read:

Then the word of the LORD came to me, saying:
"Before I formed you in the womb I knew you;
Before you were born I sanctified you;
I ordained you a prophet to the nations." (Jer. 1:4–5)

The prophet Jeremiah knew who he was. Not only did he know he was the son of Hilkiah, but, far more important, he knew he had been created by God for God's purposes.

Notice the number of times the Lord personalizes His statement to Jeremiah. He said, "I formed *you*. I knew *you*. Before *you* were born I sanctified *you*. I ordained *you*." The Lord did not consider Jeremiah to be some form of "anonymous flesh." Jeremiah was a *person*, known fully by the Lord, formed individually by God, and set apart by God for His purposes.

This understanding mirrors the truth in Psalm 139 when

David said: "Your eyes saw my substance, being yet unformed. And in Your book they all were written, the days fashioned for me, when as yet there were none of them" (Ps. 139:16).

From the womb, you are a person in God's eyes. He knows who He is creating you to be—He knows the full plan and purpose for your life, your talents, your potential skills, your desires and dreams, your personality, and every detail of your makeup as a one-of-a-kind individual.

The prophet and herald of Jesus Christ, John the Baptist, was another person who Scripture expressly says had a unique destiny from the time he was in his mother's womb. An angel spoke to Zacharias, John's father, about the baby not yet conceived: "He will be great in the sight of the Lord, and shall drink neither wine nor strong drink. *He will also be filled with the Holy Spirit, even from his mother's womb.* And he will turn many of the children of Israel to the Lord their God" (Luke 1:15–16, emphasis added).

John was not only created by God, but also indwelt by God, who designed his purpose on the earth to begin functioning before he was born.

That prophetic word to Zacharias was fulfilled. The gospel of Luke records the encounter between Mary, who was pregnant with Jesus, and her cousin Elizabeth, who was pregnant with John the Baptist. Elizabeth said, "Indeed, as soon as the voice of your greeting sounded in my ears, the babe leaped in my womb for joy" (Luke 1:44). Even in the womb, incapable of speech and other rational responses, John the Baptist was able to respond, prompted by the Spirit, to the presence of his Lord. His mother knew that he "leaped" and that his leap was "for joy" that Mary was bearing the Messiah.

The apostle Paul said of himself, "It pleased God, *who separated me from my mother's womb and called me through His grace*, to reveal His Son in me, that I might preach Him among the Gentiles" (Gal. 1:15–16, emphasis added). Paul believed that he was known fully by God and belonged fully to God from his mother's womb. His purpose was established even before his birth.

God knows who you are *from your mother's womb*. And He knows who your child is. He also knows the full destiny and purpose for each child.

What precious truths these are! What a tremendous hope we can take from these verses! God knows everything about your baby and has been intimately involved in every aspect of your baby's creation from the very moment of conception. Your child has never been beyond the loving care and concern—or the watchful eye—of the Lord. Your baby is His creation. Your baby's destiny is according to His carefully wrought plan and purpose.

God used you to bring into the reality of life the personhood of *His* child.

God is present in every conception. He is intimately involved in every moment of every life He allows to be conceived.

God superintends and guards every life He allows to exist. He places every life into the context of His eternal plan and purpose.

A Special Plan for Every Life

"But," you may say, "Jeremiah was a special case. He was a prophet and, as we know from Scripture, he grew up and obeyed God and fulfilled God's purpose for his life. David's was also a special case. He was ordained to be a king from his youth, and we know that he had a heart for God all his life. John the Baptist and the apostle Paul were special people chosen by God for special purposes. What about *my* child?"

Your child is equally special.

God has a unique plan and purpose for every child conceived. We may not understand His plan fully. We may not be able to comprehend God's purposes. But we can know with faith that our perfect God does not err. He does not allow a conception that is beyond His sovereign plan and purposes.

Let me share with you a testimony I received from a young couple in our church—Mark and Diana. Their recent letter to me is a vibrant, honest, and faith-filled testimony that God has a plan and purpose for *every* child, even the child who may be born with mental problems or physical deformities.

Centuries ago, and still today in some primitive cultures, a baby born with any kind of abnormality was left to die. The thinking was that death was better for such a child than life. Even in our society, there are those who whisper, "It's too bad her mother didn't miscarry."

Better for such a child to die? According to whom? And better

23

for whom—the parents or the child? Only God holds the authority to determine life and death. We must assume that if a child with mental or physical problems lives through birth, the Lord meant that child to be alive on this earth. The primary people who are going to benefit from the child's life are those who *care* for that child. Our sovereign Lord always has a plan and purpose for every life. And for those who belong to Him through faith in Jesus Christ, His way is *always* for our eternal good and His eternal glory. *Always!*

Mark, the baby's father, wrote:

Bethany came to us in September about five years ago. She was, as all children, a gift from the Lord. She was our third gift—our quiver was full. It was not long after she was born, however, that we became anxious. The nurses were taking too long to bathe her. We had no idea she was in the intensive care unit.

My wife, Diana, never flinched at the clamor of the ICU with all of the blinking, beeping, and shuffling going on around Bethany. She went straight to her new daughter with the same delight, admiration, and warmhearted love and affection she had shown to our other two children. I, on the other hand, needed to get a serious grip. I kept babbling on about her future and what might be involved and how we would have to approach her life.

The day after Bethany was born, she was diagnosed as a Down syndrome baby. Only the sovereignty of God held us from collapsing. We blamed each other's families, trembled and shook, and then prayed for guidance. A few days later I came to my senses through the help of more prayer in the presence of my friends. I realized that Bethany was not a syndrome but our *child*—she was a gift from our loving and wise Father.

The birth of Bethany began a wonderful journey for our family. We discovered a closer walk with God. The compassion of God moved through us as we delighted in caring for her and receiving her love. We were encouraged by the acceptance of Bethany by those in our church, and we were filled with joy and enthusiasm for Bethany's future. I could go on for pages about the special times we all shared with her, the blessings we received, the wisdom we were given, and the closeness we felt with our Savior and Lord.

As Christmas 2000 approached, the hustle and bustle of our lives intensified. We had no idea, however, that this would be the Christmas that would change our lives forever . . .

Bethany had just turned three, and what a charger she was! From a weak, frail, and sluggish baby, she had become a running, chattering, joyful little busybody! She was attending a preschool and was surrounded by friends in the church.

We knew immediately that something was wrong when Bethany awoke sad and did not feel like playing, and then that night, could not sleep and could not stop a mournful cry. We took Bethany to the urgent care facility the next day, then again on the following day, and then again two days later, which was Christmas.

None of the physicians who saw Bethany could tell us what was ailing her. It was only after many medical tests and much observation that she was diagnosed with leukemia on New Year's Eve. I lay in bed with her that night to hold her from crawling off the high hospital bed. Up to that point, her pain was so great she could not move, let alone walk. The amount of morphine they pumped into her little body was tremendous, and even so, she did not lie still until about three o'clock in the morning. Her lungs stopped from time to time that night, and nurses rushed in to jolt her back into breathing. From the day of that diagnosis, our lives intensified greatly. We became utterly dependent on help from God the Father just to get through each day.

Diana was strong in her service to Bethany and believed God would heal her baby. I felt like an empty shell. I walked with a deadened sensation in my body, yet I felt that at any moment I might burst into panic or fear. I wanted to fight, protect, and preserve the life of my little girl, and I felt completely confused and bewildered that there wasn't anything I could do to keep her from getting sicker and sicker. I was humbled to the point of feeling completely useless, even as others around me—and I as well—*expected* me to be able to act courageously, give wise counsel to my family, and serve God.

Once the holidays were over, the physicians made a "plan" for Bethany's care. We were encouraged at their prognosis that Bethany had a 90 percent chance of surviving. The physicians prescribed a course of chemotherapy that we followed for the next eleven months. The last three months we were able to administer the chemo at home. Even though Bethany lost all of her beautiful hair and had a plastic tube coming out of her chest that led right into the main vein of her heart, she had no reservations about living life cheerfully.

Bethany was scheduled to have the central line for her chemo removed in October, right after her fourth birthday. After a few weeks of double-checking the results of her ten-month chemotherapy regimen, we were crushed to find out the leukemia was back. The physicians now put her chances of survival at 30 to 50 percent.

Shortly after this, we went to Castaic Lake to enjoy the outdoors together as a family. I will never forget that day. Bethany was thrilled at the opportunity to climb the nearby hills—she refused to be carried. I could hardly fathom the grace and mercy of God as I watched my little Down syndrome girl, after ten months of chemotherapy, with her leukemia back at about 41 percent of what it had been before—having the strength and enthusiasm she had. God was teaching us to trust Him and follow His will step by step.

That night, I found Bethany sitting on the floor, busy with her toys. I sat down with her on the floor to play. She was so precious—fond memories began to flood my mind of the joyful times we had shared. I wept desperately at the thought of losing her. Bethany patted me on the head and asked, "Wha' happen, Papa? Wha' happen?" There was my little daughter cheerfully talking to me—it almost seemed to me as if she knew God's plan for her and was satisfied with it. I resolved inside my heart to give her my best and to make her life as joyful as I could.

One more chemo regimen was prescribed to blast this resistant leukemia from her body, even at the risk of damaging other organs. That was to be followed by a bone marrow transplant. Our son Christopher turned out to be a perfect match for the transplant. Our daughter Michelle was no match at all, but would have gladly given anything for her little sister.

The week of the transplant, which turned out to be the last week of Bethany's life, is like a blur to me. I do recall Diana calling me as she did her utmost to help Bethany breathe and rest comfortably. When I arrived at the hospital after her call, I found Bethany sitting under an oxygen tent, and for the first time, she seemed to give up on life. When she was intubated—a tube inserted past her throat down into her lungs—the look on her face cried out silently for help. The tube caused her to cough and gasp for air, yet no sound could be heard because the lungs needed air to make a coughing noise. I also remember the sound of Diana crying out in her love, "Bethany, please don't leave me," as Bethany slipped away from us. In the end, Bethany's little heart failed, like an athlete who had run far past his limit. All the clamor of the ICU room gave way to only the sound of our own moans and sobbing. The cries of our children as we told them Bethany would no longer walk with us here on earth are indelibly planted in our hearts.

Bethany's fight against leukemia had lasted sixteen months—from Christmas Day to Easter week.

Bethany left this world in much the same way she entered it—hooked up to tubes, wires, needles, respirators, monitors, and many attending hands and watchful eyes carefully monitoring her delicate life balances. For the greater part of her life, however, Bethany lived free of these things. We choose to remember how she *lived* more than how she died. She loved playing games and singing songs with her sister Michelle and brother Christopher. She was a fun little trickster who enjoyed books and gardening, coloring, and animals.

There were times throughout Bethany's life and illness that we asked God, "What have we done? What haven't we done?" We felt ourselves grappling with the issue of sin and whether something we had done or failed to do had contributed to Bethany's illness. There are no answers to those questions, and we always came to the point of finding our faithfulness wanting and God's faithfulness increasing infinitely toward us.

Bethany now enjoys God face-to-face and is perfectly satisfied with the life that she lived on this earth for only four and a half years. We tell our children that Bethany took the fast track to heaven—a rocket ship to fly her journey. We are still on the wagon train of life. God alone decides the length of our journey and the speed at which we travel it. We encourage ourselves as a family that Bethany is in the presence of almighty God, with no pain or tears and no anxiety about missing us. She is no longer a four and a half year old, Down syndrome girl. She is whole, complete, and fully mature in the Lord! We have absolutely no doubt that we will see her again, even as we will see God and His Son, Jesus, face-to-face. It is only then that we will truly understand all of His purposes for Bethany's life, but we know this: Our praise to God will be for eternity that His wisdom and holiness are perfect.

Our struggles, of course, didn't end with Bethany's death. We still struggle to get through holidays without her. We still struggle with trying to understand what has happened in the weakness of our own logic. We still struggle with being submissive to God's plan and serving Him joyfully until the day He calls each of us home to Himself. Even so, if He asked us to go through this all again—knowing what we now know—we also know we would be willing to do so for the sake of knowing Him as we do today. He is a God of infinite grace, mercy, compassion, and peace.

The following is an excerpt from the eulogy Mark gave at Bethany's memorial service:

I believe Bethany was sent by our great God to teach us the character of His unconditional love . . . To Bethany, things like Down syndrome, leukemia, chemotherapy, and bone marrow transplants were trivial. If you entered into her life—whether at home or in a hospital room—she would be overjoyed to greet you and equally enthusiastic when you left.

When we prayed, Bethany would have it no other way than for all of us to join hands. Her trust was great and she lived without regrets. When she felt she needed to repent, she would drop to the floor with her hands on her face.

Diana often sang with Bethany, "He who began a good work in you will be faithful to complete it." Bethany is now complete and full of purest joy. We can almost picture her singing praises to our holy God.

If Bethany could speak right now, I feel confident she may well say, "Do not sorrow, for the joy of the LORD is your strength" (Neh. 8:10).

Let me ask you:

Was Bethany a *person*?

Did God know everything about Bethany even before Bethany's conception?

Was God actively involved in her life?

Did God have full knowledge of her—a knowledge that continues to this day?

Did God have unlimited understanding about every detail of Bethany's life?

Was God Bethany's personal Creator?

Had God personally planned Bethany's eternal destiny?

The answer to each of these questions is a resounding "Yes!"

God had a special, unique, highly personal, powerful purpose for Bethany's life on this earth. Her life greatly influenced not only the lives of her parents and siblings, but the entire life of the church community surrounding her family. Her life touched the lives of the doctors, nurses, and other hospital workers who cared for her, as well as her neighbors and the friends she made wherever she went. Her life is touching *your* life today as you read her story—as it did mine while knowing her!

Bethany was not a "syndrome" of any kind, as her father so wisely stated. She was a gift of the Father to this world.

The same is true for your life and the life of your child.

The first and foremost thing we can conclude with certainty about a child is this: *Every child conceived is a God-created and God-loved person with a God-given purpose and destiny.*

Let your comfort begin with that truth. God created your child. God loved your child and continues to love your child. God's purpose and destiny for your child are fulfilled perfectly, even if the child dies. The reality of that is beyond anything you can know fully this side of heaven.

THREE

How Does God Regard Children?

THROUGHOUT SCRIPTURE, THE LORD'S HEART SEEMS especially tender toward children.

One of the most endearing passages in all the Bible is found in Ezekiel 16. The Lord describes how He picked up the Israelites as if they were an infant abandoned in a field:

> As for your nativity, on the day you were born your navel cord was not cut, nor were you washed in water to cleanse you; you were not rubbed with salt nor wrapped in swaddling cloths. No eye pitied you, to do any of these things for you, to have compassion on you; but you were thrown out into the open field, when you yourself were loathed on the day you were born.
>
> And when I passed by you and saw you struggling in your own blood, I said to you in your blood, "Live!" Yes, I said to you in your blood, "Live!" I made you thrive like a plant in the field; and you grew, matured, and became very beautiful. (Ezek. 16:4–7)

God made it very clear that He had called Israel to be His own from its origin. He had loved His people from their infancy, like an orphaned and exposed baby. What was true metaphorically for Israel is true for all children who are His. His gracious love for the little ones is the fitting picture of His love for Israel.

Scripture reaffirms again and again two great truths:

- God considers all babies to be His.
- God loves all who are His "innocent little ones."

All Babies Are "Owned" by God

God's great judgment on His people was never voiced more clearly than through the prophet Ezekiel later in that same chapter. His indictment of the people of Jerusalem was extremely strong:

You took your sons and your daughters, whom you bore to Me, and these you sacrificed to them to be devoured. Were your acts of harlotry a small matter, that you have slain My children and offered them up to them by causing them to pass through the fire? And in all your abominations and acts of harlotry you did not remember the days of your youth, when you were naked and bare, struggling in your blood. (Ezek. 16:20–22)

God lays full claim to these innocent sons and daughters who are sacrificed to false gods. He says these children were born to

Him and they are His children. He exerts full ownership over the innocent ones. He even refers to them as "the innocents" in Jeremiah 2:34 and 19:4. Though fallen creatures like all Adam's offspring, infants are not culpable in the same sense as those whose sins are willful and premeditated. Therefore God expresses serious displeasure over the people of Israel, who failed to treat their little ones the way God treated them.

For His innocent ones, God feels great compassion! We see this clearly in the story of Jonah.

When the Lord called the prophet Jonah to go to Nineveh and preach repentance, Jonah did so, but very reluctantly. Jonah had no desire to see the people of this enemy city turn to his God or see God bestow any mercy on them. He hated Gentiles in general, and Ninevites in particular. Jonah would have preferred that God wipe out the entire city. A stormy trip on the high seas, an experience in the belly of a great fish, and several days of preaching in Nineveh later, Jonah felt he had fulfilled God's mandate on his life, but he wasn't happy about the success he had experienced in calling the Ninevites to repentance. Jonah actually resented God's choosing to forgive the repentant Ninevites. God responded to Jonah's displeasure by saying:

And should I not pity Nineveh, that great city, in which are more than one hundred and twenty thousand persons who cannot discern between their right hand and their left—and much livestock? (Jonah 4:11)

Those who could not tell their left hand from their right were the little children and those who were mentally disabled and therefore incapable of making such a judgment. These innocent children in Nineveh, as well as the animals, were clearly objects of God's pity. God restrained His judgment on Nineveh because Nineveh repented, so that wholesale destruction on the innocent children was avoided.

God Alone Determines Age of Accountability

The question naturally arises, "Who qualifies for God's compassion as an innocent infant or child?"

In certain church circles, the question is often couched in this way: "What is the age of accountability?"

The issue is not truly one of "age" but rather "condition."

I have baptized young people who have told me that they believe they were saved at the age of ten, or twelve, or eight. There is no one age at which *every* person suddenly becomes accountable for knowing the difference between sin and righteousness, judgment and forgiveness, and understanding the gospel. All children are unique in their development and exposure to the truth. There is no one age in the Bible at which all children are declared to be "accountable." Neither is there one chronological age in a person's life in which a person suddenly and automatically knows right from wrong or is capable of understanding God's plan for salvation.

The condition of accountability is what matters. Every infant or child who dies before reaching a condition of moral culpability goes instantly to heaven at death.

A child who has not reached moral culpability is a child who has not reached sufficient mature understanding to comprehend convincingly the issues of law and grace, sin and salvation. Only God knows the time when a child becomes "accountable." The reason Scripture includes one account of Jesus between His infancy and adulthood, at the age of twelve, is to show that He had come to a full understanding of His divine nature and His personal mission. When He told His earthly parents, who had been looking for Him, "I must be about My Father's business," He was informing them, at the age of twelve, of His full awareness of the realities of His life as the Son of God. And that is a good general age to look for the condition of accountability.

The Condition of Accountability

A child who has not reached moral culpability is a child who has not reached sufficient mature understanding to comprehend convincingly the issues of law and grace, sin and salvation.

A miscarried or aborted baby has no understanding of law and grace, sin and salvation. Neither does a baby who dies at birth or shortly thereafter. Neither does an infant. Neither does a toddler or young child—or even an older child, in some cases.

At some point in a child's maturation, he or she comes to have an understanding of law and grace. In other words, the child begins to comprehend and *understand* these principles:

God has rules and commandments; sin involves the violation or breaking of God's laws; forgiveness of sin has been made possible through the death of Jesus Christ on the cross; the grace of God allows for all who believe in and receive Jesus Christ as their Savior and submit to Him as Lord to be cleansed of their sin and live in the newness of life and joyful obedience to Him.

From child to child, that precise age varies. It is the "condition" that counts, not a calendar.

Some children, of course, never reach such a level of maturation. They are mentally impaired to the point that they are forever locked into thinking as a young child thinks—we might say they "have the mind of a five-year-old" or they are "like a child" in their mental capacities related to reasoning, remembering, or making moral choices. Their bodies may mature fully, but their minds do not. These, too, are "children" who may never reach a condition of moral culpability.

Children in a Heathen Culture Are "Innocents"

Sometimes the question arises whether the children of unbelievers are received by God as His unique possessions in the same way as infants from Christian homes. Some apparently imagine that infants whose parents are believers are safe because of the parents' faith, but infants from heathen cultures are condemned for their parents' sins. On the contrary, Scripture clearly teaches that the children of idolatrous parents are also considered "innocent" in God's eyes until they reach a state of moral culpability.

In the days of the prophet Jeremiah, those who followed false gods in the land of Israel were guilty of offering their children as burnt sacrifices. God spoke of His judgment on those who followed this horrific practice, at the same time calling the sacrificed children "innocent." We read in Jeremiah 19:4–7:

> Because they have forsaken Me and made this an alien place, because they have burned incense in it to other gods whom neither they, their fathers, nor the kings of Judah have known, and have filled this place with the blood of the *innocents* (they have also built the high places of Baal, to burn their sons with fire for burnt offerings to Baal, which I did not command or speak, nor did it come into My mind) . . . I will make void the counsel of Judah and Jerusalem in this place, and I will cause them to fall by the sword before their enemies and by the hands of those who seek their lives. (emphasis added)

Some time ago, I attended a medical conference and the question arose about whether infants go immediately and directly to heaven. Many of those in attendance were missionaries, including missionary doctors and nurses who work in pagan Third World nations. These medical professionals see a great deal of infant death, including miscarriages and death at birth. For the most part, these doctors and nurses are working in idolatrous, pagan countries.

One neonatal nurse came to me after my presentation. She worked in a very difficult environment, mostly with premature babies. She told me that she had never known fully what to say to the parents of babies who died. Her joy was almost overwhelming as I explained to her more fully what I believe the Bible teaches about the death of all babies, even those whose parents practice the most satanic and godless religions. She said, "At last I have hope for these little ones! At last I can convey that hope to their parents, even if they do not yet know the Lord!"

In reality, in the broad history of the world, the vast majority of those who have died prior to reaching full moral accountability have been those who were conceived by unsaved parents! Literally billions of babies have been conceived and then miscarried, died in infancy, or died in childbirth in areas of the world unreached by the gospel or in areas where a false religion holds people in an evil grip. God does not use the word *innocent* unless He means it. The sacrificed children of Baal worshipers were not cursed or held guilty along with their parents for evil rejection of the true God. Though the parents were guilty, the little ones were innocent. God is just and will not punish the innocent.

Millions upon millions of babies and children in undeveloped countries and pagan cultures have died through the centuries. Millions upon millions of babies conceived by parents who were Hindus, Buddhists, Muslims, atheists, or followers of any one of thousands of cults and false religions have died. These children are also "innocents" in God's eyes.

The Scripture weighs very heavily toward the fact that innocent children are in heaven, redeemed and dwelling in the presence of God. In Revelation, we read that in heaven we will find people "out of every tribe and tongue and people and nation" (Rev. 5:9). There are tribes and tongues today—the so-called "people groups" of various isolated and distinctive ethnicities, cultures, and languages—who have never heard the gospel. Yet God's Word says representatives of those tribes and tongues will be in heaven. How is this possible? One way is through the redemption of their little ones. These will be among those who are made "kings and priests to our God" (Rev. 5:10).

Babies Do Not Pay for the Sins of Their Parents

Those who question the innocence of babies in heathen cultures tend to hold an opinion that babies are an "extension" of their parents' beliefs and, thus, are in some way culpable for the sins of their parents. That is not what Scripture teaches us.

What does the Lord mean, then, in Exodus 20:5, where He says, "I, the LORD your God, am a jealous God, visiting the iniquity of the fathers upon the children to the third and fourth generations of those who hate Me"? Also, when the Lord met Moses on Sinai to give him the Ten Commandments on tablets of stone, He announced His arrival by saying, "The LORD, the LORD God, merciful and gracious, longsuffering, and abounding in goodness and truth, keeping mercy for thousands, forgiving iniquity and transgression and sin, by no means clearing the guilty, visiting the iniquity of the fathers upon the children and the children's children to the third and fourth generation" (Exod. 34:6–7; see also Deut. 5:9 and Jer. 32:18). Doesn't that mean children are held guilty for the sins of their parents?

No. In fact, Deuteronomy 24:16 says, "Fathers shall not be put to death for their children, nor shall children be put to death for their fathers; a person shall be put to death for his own sin." The principle underlying that law is given in Ezekiel 18:20: "The soul who sins shall die. The son shall not bear the guilt of the father, nor the father bear the guilt of the son. The righteousness of the righteous shall be upon himself, and the wickedness of the wicked shall be upon himself." That is an emphatic denial that a child is held guilty for the sins of the parents.

Are these contradictory? No. No son bears the *guilt* of his father. But the children of a sinful generation are powerfully affected by the *consequences* of the sins of a society.

In Exodus, God was giving the law and warning the fathers of Israel that if they did not worship Him alone, but turned to idols, they would corrupt the population spiritually, and that would have evil consequences for generations. The idolatry of the fathers would naturally infect succeeding generations. Once spiritual pollution was set in motion in Israel, it would be so pervasive that it would foul the stream into generations of children, grandchildren, and great-grandchildren. Israel's subsequent history demonstrated the truth of that warning. Sin begets more sin, and the pervasive effect of a father's bad example is often passed down for generations.

But God is not saying that he blames children for their fathers' sins. The *consequences* (not the *guilt*) of the sin are visited on the children. Moreover, the cycle of idolatry and its consequences can be broken when a younger generation turns to God in repentant faith. Notice that God expressly says he visits the fathers' iniquities "to the third and fourth generation *of those who hate [Him]*." When children follow the sins of their fathers, the evil consequences are multiplied across the generations. But whatever *guilt* the children may bear is their own guilt for following in their father's sins. Notice that no threat is ever made against children who mature to love God, suggesting that *they* might be visited with the sins of their fathers.

So Exodus 20:5 does not contradict Ezekiel 18:20. Both are true. When a generation is sinful and disobedient to God, subsequent generations can reap disastrous consequences from that—and those consequences are multiplied greatly if they follow in their parents' sins. But children are not held responsible for their parents' sins.

Rather, Scripture says that babies do *not* have culpability for the sins of their parents. That fact was clearly stated by the Lord through Moses as He told the Israelites what would happen to them in the aftermath of their disbelief and disobedience shortly after crossing the Red Sea. Let me remind you of the background to God's statement to them.

When the children of Israel came out of Egypt, God's plan was for them to enter the Land of Promise within a matter of weeks. The Israelites sent spies into the land, however, and with the exception of Caleb and Joshua, the spies reported back that the land was impossible for them to conquer. With fruit in their hands as evidence, the spies reported that the land was a good land. But then, they went on to report that the people were "greater and taller" and that the cities were "great and fortified up to heaven" and occupied by giants. Ten of the spies were terrified at the prospect of going up against these people, and the Israelites followed their lead and refused to enter the land (Deut. 1:19–33).

God was angry with His people. He had promised to go before them and fight for them and deliver the land into their hands, just as He had sovereignly delivered them from Egypt. Their disbelief in the Lord's ability to do this resulted in His vowing, "Surely not one of these men of this evil generation shall see that good land of which I swore to give to your fathers, except Caleb the son of Jephunneh; he shall see it, and to him and his children I am giving the land on which he walked, because he wholly followed the LORD." The Lord also said, "Joshua the son of Nun, who stands before you, he shall go in there. Encourage him, for he shall cause Israel to inherit it." He concluded, "But as for you, turn and take your journey into the wilderness by the Way of the Red Sea" (Deut. 1:34–38, 40).

The Lord declared this, however, about the infants and young children: "Moreover your little ones and your children, who you say will be victims, who today have no knowledge of good and evil, they shall go in there; to them I will give it, and they shall possess it" (Deut. 1:39).

The Israelite children of sinful parents were allowed to enter fully into the blessing God had for His people. They were in no way held accountable, responsible, or punishable for the sins of their parents. Why? Because they had no knowledge of good and evil, right or wrong.

In Ezekiel 18:20, the Lord says, "The soul who sins shall die. The son shall not bear the guilt of the father, nor the father bear the guilt of the son. The righteousness of the righteous shall be upon himself, and the wickedness of the wicked shall be upon himself."

The same is true today.

A child may be conceived out of wedlock.

A fetus may be aborted by an ungodly mother.

A child may be beaten to death by an ungodly father.

But before God, that child does not bear culpability for the sins of the parents.

The children were considered "innocent" of sin. *They* had not rebelled; they had no "say" regarding the Israelite's rebellion and unbelief. In a profound way, God blessed their innocence.

What About All Heathen People?

Let me digress for just a moment to cover an issue that is related to the innocence of heathen children.

It is very important to understand at this point what I am *not* saying. This innocence is limited to children (and the mentally deficient) and does not include anyone else. To help you see that this is a limited consideration by God, I have to reject those who want to open this door of innocence, which is limited by God to those precious "little ones," to include all heathen adults who do not have a biblical understanding of sin and righteousness, right and wrong, good and evil. That is not a position that can be supported by Scripture. In fact, the very opposite is true. The apostle Paul wrote about this very issue in the opening statements of his letter to the Romans:

> I am not ashamed of the gospel of Christ, for it is the power of God to salvation for everyone who believes, for the Jew first and also for the Greek. For in it the righteousness of God is revealed from faith to faith; as it is written, "The just shall live by faith."
>
> For the wrath of God is revealed from heaven against all ungodliness and unrighteousness of men, who suppress the truth in unrighteousness, because what may be known of God is manifest in them, for God has shown it to them. For since the creation of the world His invisible attributes are clearly seen, being understood by the things that are made, even His eternal power and Godhead, so that they are without excuse, because, although they knew God, they did not glorify Him as God, nor were thankful, but became futile in their thoughts, and their foolish hearts were darkened. Professing to be wise, they became fools, and changed the glory of the incorruptible God into an image made like corruptible man—and birds and four-footed animals and creeping things.

Therefore God also gave them up to uncleanness, in the lusts of their hearts, to dishonor their bodies among themselves, who exchanged the truth of God for the lie, and worshiped and served the creature rather than the Creator, who is blessed forever. Amen.

For this reason God gave them up to vile passions . . . And even as they did not like to retain God in their knowledge, God gave them over to a debased mind, to do those things which are not fitting; being filled with all unrighteousness, sexual immorality, wickedness, covetousness, maliciousness; full of envy, murder, strife, deceit, evil-mindedness; they are whisperers, backbiters, haters of God, violent, proud, boasters, inventors of evil things, disobedient to parents, undiscerning, untrustworthy, unloving, unforgiving, unmerciful; who, knowing the righteous judgment of God, that those who practice such things are deserving of death, not only do the same but also approve of those who practice them.

Therefore you are inexcusable, O man, whoever you are who judge, for in whatever you judge another you condemn yourself; for you who judge practice the same things. (Rom. 1:16–2:1)

According to that passage, everyone has an innate, rudimentary knowledge of God. Rather than respond to that knowledge, people choose to follow their own imaginations, create their own gods, and worship them instead of their Creator. Heathen adults are responsible to follow the truth of God to an understanding of the gospel and respond to it with faith. Their failure to do so is accounted to them as an act of willful defiance or rebellion. They are inexcusable because they are capable of discerning good from evil, and they willfully choose what is evil. Heathen adults who die are therefore morally culpable for their sin in a way that infants who die are not.

A Proper Burial for Jeroboam's Baby

The truth that a baby is not culpable for the parents' sin is also displayed in the story of King Jeroboam and his baby boy.

King Jeroboam was a wicked king. He multiplied idols throughout the land, and it was under his rule that the priests to these false gods instituted the burning of children as sacrifices. The Lord said very plainly and directly to Jeroboam through the prophet Ahijah,

You have done more evil than all who were before you, for you have gone and made for yourself other gods and molded images to provoke Me to anger, and have cast Me behind your back—therefore behold! I will bring disaster on the house of Jeroboam, and will cut off from Jeroboam every male in Israel, bond and free; I will take away the remnant of the house of Jeroboam, as one takes away refuse until it is all gone. The dogs shall eat whoever belongs to Jeroboam and dies in the city, and the birds of the air shall eat whoever dies in the field; for the LORD has spoken! (1 Kings 14:9–11)

All Jeroboam's heirs and relatives were sentenced to death by God. Not only that, but they were sentenced to the worst death known in Israel at that time—a death without proper burial. The worst desecration possible was to have one's body ripped apart by wild animals and scavenging birds. The Lord said through His prophet that all of Jeroboam's male relatives would be swept away as refuse, the wild dogs of the city and the vultures of the field eating their dead bodies where they fell. Except for one male heir.

The infant son of Jeroboam was spared this horrible, ghastly death. The Lord said to Jeroboam, "Arise therefore, go to your own house. When your feet enter the city, the child shall die. And all Israel shall mourn for him and bury him, for he is the only one of Jeroboam who shall come to the grave, because in him there is found something good toward the LORD God of Israel in the house of Jeroboam" (1 Kings 14:12–13).

Jeroboam's infant son was to die along with Jeroboam's other heirs, but his death was not to be the same. He would die a seemingly natural death the moment Jeroboam's feet entered the city. His death would be mourned, and he would be given a burial befitting a prince. The Lord noted that in this infant son there would be "found something good toward the LORD God of Israel."

That little child had no righteous merit in himself—he had done nothing to warrant the label "righteous." Nor had he willfully done anything to warrant the label "unrighteous." He had not rebelled against the Lord God. He had participated in no worship ceremonies to a false god. What was the "something good" found in him? Scripture doesn't say. Childlike humility, perhaps. Maybe he had a childish revulsion to the pagan rituals. Whatever it was, it was nothing that was meritorious for salvation (Rom. 8:7–8); but God, being gracious, set His favor on the child and preserved him from the dishonorable death that represented divine judgment against those who had willfully participated in Jeroboam's sin. As a result, he was given an honorable death and burial, and he went immediately into the presence of the Lord.

Mercy for the Babies of God's Enemies

The question may arise among those who are familiar with the Bible: "What about the death at God's command of the babies of enemies? After all, even though Jeroboam's son was spared the indignity of being eaten by scavengers, he nonetheless died. God did not spare his life." In fact, there are other passages in the Bible in which God seems to authorize the death of infants as part of His judgment on a wicked nation.

For example, when God called for judgment upon Babylon, He spoke through the prophet Isaiah: "Their children also will be dashed to pieces before their eyes" (Isa. 13:16).

When God called for Assyria to make a war of judgment against Israel, He said through the prophet Hosea:

Samaria is held guilty,
For she has rebelled against her God.

50

They shall fall by the sword,
Their infants shall be dashed in pieces,
And their women with child ripped open. (Hos. 13:16)

The same was said of Assyria's war on Egypt:

She was carried away,
She went into captivity;
Her young children also were dashed to pieces
At the head of every street. (Nah. 3:10)

The following verses from the Psalms are amazing—they speak of *joy* being felt by those who killed the young children of Babylonian captors:

O daughter of Babylon, who are to be destroyed,
Happy the one who repays you as you have served us!
Happy the one who takes and dashes
Your little ones against the rock! (Ps. 137:8–9)

The first response of many who read these verses is to recoil in shock. It is painful and disturbing to read about little ones being dashed against a rock, let alone someone being blessed for doing so. These passages are part of the inspired Word of God, however, so we must deal with them. So, how is it that we can square the argument that God loves and has compassion on His innocent ones, and at the same time accept the fact that God foretells of children being "dashed to pieces" as part of the conquest of those who come against His people?

The only way these two seemingly opposite perspectives can be reconciled is this: *Children experience a better life after their deaths than they would if they were allowed to mature to adulthood on this earth.* The death of the innocent heathen may seem disastrous to the adults who live on this earth, but from God's point of view, their death is a blessing. The life they experience with Him in eternity so far surpasses any good they may have experienced on this earth that there truly is no comparison. Scripture clearly expresses this belief in a glorious hereafter for a young child who dies.

A Better Life Than This Life

Job experienced such intense despair that he opened his mouth and "cursed the day of his birth." He said, "May the day perish on which I was born, and the night in which it was said, 'A male child is conceived.' May that day be darkness; may God above not seek it, nor the light shine upon it. May darkness and the shadow of death claim it; may a cloud settle on it; may the blackness of the day terrify it" (Job 3:1–5).

Whatever could go wrong did go wrong in Job's life. His wife advised him to curse God and die. He didn't listen to her. Scripture tells us, "Job did not sin with his lips" (Job 2:9–10). Job did, however, express how he *felt* in the aftermath of the tremendous loss of his family and possessions, and in his being afflicted from head to toe with painful boils. He said:

Why did I not die at birth?
Why did I not perish when I came from the womb?
Why did the knees receive me?
Or why the breasts, that I should nurse?
For now I would have lain still and been quiet,
I would have been asleep;
Then I would have been at rest
With kings and counselors of the earth,
Who built ruins for themselves,
Or with princes who had gold,
Who filled their houses with silver;
Or why was I not hidden like a stillborn child,
Like infants who never saw light?
There the wicked cease from troubling,
And there the weary are at rest.
There the prisoners rest together;
They do not hear the voice of the oppressor.
The small and great are there,
And the servant is free from his master. (Job 3:11–19)

Job describes a paradise for the stillborn child! He compares his life of misery, sorrow, and oppression with that of the stillborn child and concludes the stillborn child is better off. Such a little one is free from all strife, all torment, all pain and suffering, and all bondage.

Job was the most righteous man on earth at that time. He was God's man—with a sound theology and a sound faith. Job believed in life after death and expressed that confidence when he said: "And after my skin is destroyed, this I know, that in my flesh I shall see God, whom I shall see for myself, and my eyes shall behold, and not another" (19:26–27). So Job believed in resurrection life in which he could be in the Lord's presence. Here he indicates that hope is valid for a stillborn child. And he concluded he would have been better off if he had been stillborn and gone right into God's presence to be at "rest" in the life to come.

The stillborn child lives with the formerly weary and the formerly captive and the formerly oppressed. Job certainly wasn't describing hell because the one trademark of hell is a place of no rest where wickedness abounds, and Job described the life of the stillborn in the hereafter as a life of rest that is free from wickedness.

Job's pain and suffering were so deep that he wished the day had never come for him to be born. He said, "Why did I not die at birth? Why did I not perish when I came from the womb?" (Job 3:11).

He went on to say:

> Why was I not hidden like a stillborn child,
> Like infants who never saw light?
> There the wicked cease from troubling,
> And there the weary are at rest. (Job 3:16–17)

Job believed he would have been *far better off* if he had been miscarried or stillborn. He believed that if he had died before birth, he would have experienced a better life than anything this life had to offer him—life in the presence of his living Redeemer (19:25).

By the time Job said that, he had known the best of times. As a blameless and godly man, he had seven sons and three daughters. He had thousands of sheep, camels, oxen, donkeys. He had a vast household of possessions and servants. God had "blessed the work of his hands" in all ways. (See Job 1:1–3, 10.)

Job had also known the worst of times. His flocks and herds had been stolen, and his servants had been slaughtered by a marauding band of thieves. His sons and daughters had all died under a collapsed roof. He had developed painful boils "from the sole of his foot to the crown of his head" (Job 2:7).

Job knew that life—even a good, full life—is always marked by a degree of trouble, difficult decisions, personality conflicts, natural disasters, power struggles, hard choices, the pain of suffering, and the rises and falls of various trends and tides. To die as an infant, however, would be to experience nothing but "rest"—a life unmarked and untainted by any twinge of misery, bitterness, difficulty, oppression, or bondage. He said that in the paradise to come, there is only freedom, joy, and "ease" (Job 3:18–26).

In his writings, King Solomon echoed this understanding that the stillborn or miscarried child experiences the repose of paradise:

> If a man begets a hundred children and lives many years, so that the days of his years are many, but his soul is not satisfied with goodness, or indeed he has no burial, I say that a

stillborn child is better than he—for it comes in vanity and departs in darkness, and its name is covered with darkness. Though it has not seen the sun or known anything, this has more rest than that man, even if he lives a thousand years twice—but has not seen goodness. (Eccl. 6:3–6)

In essence, Solomon stated that the stillborn child has an existence that is far better than that of a long-lived person *unless* that mature person has a soul that knows and experiences the goodness of God.

In both Job and Ecclesiastes, the implication is very clear that the miscarried or stillborn baby enters a state of peace—an existence much preferred to a life marked by wickedness and trouble in this world.

This belief has been expressed throughout the ages by notable Christian theologians and writers. John Newton (1725–1807), the slave trader who became a gospel minister and wrote perhaps the most famous hymn of all time, "Amazing Grace," was certain of this truth. He wrote to close friends whose young child had died: "I hope you are both well reconciled to the death of your child. I cannot be sorry for the death of infants. How many storms do they escape! Nor can I doubt, in my private judgment, that they are included in the election of grace."[1]

Jesus Held Children in High Regard!

If we truly want to know how God regards children, we need look no farther than the lap of Jesus.

One day Jesus called a little child to Himself, set that child in the midst of His disciples, and then said, "Assuredly, I say to you, unless you are converted and become as little children, you will by no means enter the kingdom of heaven. Therefore whoever humbles himself as this little child is the greatest in the kingdom of heaven. Whoever receives one little child like this in My name receives Me" (Matt. 18:3–5).

Jesus had great regard for the status of the child. He saw in a child the model of dependency and trust, the mind of innocence and humility. He saw a person eager to please and give thanks, quick to express love, and quick to receive and obey what was commanded and taught. So He used a child for the purpose of analogy—to teach His disciples dependency, trust, humility, affection, and obedience. A child was His best illustration of the redeemed believer, who was in the kingdom of salvation.

Jesus also said, "Take heed that you do not despise one of these little ones, for I say to you that in heaven their angels always see the face of My Father who is in heaven" (Matt. 18:10). In so many ways, Jesus likened our becoming believers to becoming like children—being born again spiritually as a child is born, naked and unassuming and totally vulnerable and dependent on the Creator. Jesus never ridiculed a person for crying out to the Father like a child, or for desiring to be protected and loved by the Father as a child longs to be protected and loved. In fact, all through the Bible our Lord invites us to come as children under His tender care.

Jesus taught that we are to watch out with special care for

those who are the spiritual "children" in our midst—in the same manner that we would watch out for our physical children. If they stray, we are to go after them. If they lose their way, we are to find them and return them to the fold. No parent with six children is going to discover one of them missing from the dinner table and callously say, "Oh well, we still have five more." No—a search will be made until that missing child is found. We must do the same for the spiritually immature who pursue error.

Later in this same teaching, Jesus said this: "Even so it is not the will of your Father who is in heaven that one of these little ones should perish" (Matt. 18:14). The analogy of this statement is unmistakable. Jesus was saying that God no more wants a spiritual child to perish eternally than God wants a natural child to perish eternally. The spiritual teaching is possible only because of the underlying truth of the "natural" teaching. The analogy works, and works perfectly, only because the underlying premise is that God protects and preserves the little ones who enter His presence. Therefore, we must be diligent to protect and preserve those who spiritually enter the kingdom as little children.

Jesus repeated this teaching on another occasion when He was surrounded by a great multitude of people who were following Him and being healed by Him. Some in the multitude began to bring their children to Jesus so He might put His hands on them and pray for them. The disciples rebuked these parents, thinking the children unworthy of the same attention and regard that Jesus had been giving to the adults, and especially to those adults in great need. Jesus in turn rebuked His disciples for turning the children away. He said, "Let the little children come to Me, and do not forbid them; for of such is the kingdom of heaven" (Matt. 19:14; Mark 10:14; Luke 18:16).

"But," you may say, "Jesus was only using the children as an analogy for the way adults are converted and become part of the kingdom of God." Let me quickly point out to you that an analogy works only if it is rooted in truth! If children are not readily and fully received into the kingdom of heaven, the analogy to spiritual conversion would be a very poor one. As it is, the analogy is a great one! Children are readily accepted into the kingdom, and because of that, we are wise to become like children in our spiritual dependency upon the Lord so that we, too, might be readily accepted.

In the version of this incident recorded in the gospel of Mark, we read that Jesus instructed His disciples, "Let the little children come to Me, and do not forbid them; for of such is the kingdom of God" (Mark 10:14). Jesus then took the children up in His arms, laid His hands on them, and blessed them (Mark 10:16). I don't know of any place in the New Testament in which Jesus blesses "nonbelievers." There's no place in which Jesus blesses the "cursed" or the "damned," or indiscriminately blesses those who may be some strange hybrid of good and evil. These were real children Jesus was holding in His arms, and He said of them, "Of such is the kingdom of God" (Mark 10:14). Jesus blessed those in His arms because from heaven's perspective, they were counted among the blessed righteous ones whose rightful eternal home was heaven.

The disciples were dead wrong to assume that the heavenly kingdom is void of children. The exact opposite is true—heaven has been well populated by children who died in the womb, at birth, shortly after birth, in their young childhood, or who never developed beyond the mental capacity of children.

John Calvin once wrote in a commentary on this biblical passage, "Those little children have not yet any understanding to desire His blessing, but when they are presented to Him, He gently and kindly receives them, and dedicates them to the Father by a solemn act of blessing." Calvin went on to say, "It would be too cruel" to exclude that age from the grace of redemption. Then he wrote that it is presumption and sacrilege (an irreligious audacity) to drive far from the fold of Christ those whom He cherishes in His bosom, and to shut the door, and exclude as strangers, those whom He does not wish to be forbidden to come to Him.[2]

The great nineteenth-century Presbyterian preacher Charles Hodge wrote, "He tells us, 'Of such is the kingdom of heaven,' as though heaven was in great measure composed of the souls of redeemed infants."

Calvin and Hodge, of course, are not unique in their interpretation of this passage. The comments here mirror what many respected teachers of Christ's words have written through the ages. Jesus clearly saw innocent children as being openly and lovingly embraced by His heavenly Father.

God's Tender and Loving Regard for Children

How blessed we are to know from Scripture the affectionate regard God the Father has for children! As you think of a precious child who has died, rest in these truths:

1. God claims ownership of the little ones from every culture, tribe, nation, and people.

2. God always shows compassion on those He regards as His innocent ones.

3. In certain circumstances, God's compassion on His innocent ones is expressed through death and their coming to dwell with Him in eternity, rather than in allowing their life to continue on this earth and perhaps end in eternal punishment.

4. All children who die live in the presence of the Lord for all eternity. They are blessed forever in their death!

FOUR

What If My Child Is Not Among the Elect?

FIVE WORDS CHANGED PAULETTE'S LIFE FOREVER. HER twelve-year-old son, Roger, rushed through the back screen door into the kitchen where she was washing dishes and cried, "Peter fell into the well!"

Paulette didn't even stop to dry her hands. She quickly raced outside after her son, calling to her daughter Maggie, "Go get your father. He's in the back forty."

All the way to the well, Paulette realized she was saying the same words over and over, "No . . . no . . . no. Not again. No . . . no . . . no. Not again."

It had been three years earlier that she and her family had taken a day away from the farm chores that occupied them eighteen hours a day, almost every day of the year. They had gone to Spruce Creek for a picnic and a day of fishing. Spruce Creek was high in the mountains about an hour's drive away. At times the rapidly flowing mountain creek seemed to be bursting with trout. Word had circulated that this was one of those times, so Paulette and her husband, George, had packed a big picnic basket and bundled their family of three boys and two girls into the old truck and headed for the hills. George was hoping for a good family fish fry at the end of the day.

Sure enough, the fish were biting. Two of the boys—Roger and Bill—had left the rest of the family to move a little farther upstream. "Be careful," Paulette called after them. "Some of those rocks are pretty slippery. And stay in sight!"

The boys did as they were told, and through the brush, Paulette could see them, about fifty feet away, dropping their poles into the creek. Occasionally she heard their squeals of delight as they pulled a fish from the water.

According to Roger, who was nine years old at the time, it was a slippery rock that started the disaster. Billy, age seven, decided he wanted to try fishing from the other side of the creek. As he crossed the creek on a tree trunk that had fallen over the creek, he slipped and fell into the water. His left foot became wedged between two rocks. With great effort, he was able to keep his head above water as he called to his brother for help and tried to maneuver himself to free his foot from the rocks. Roger saw what happened and immediately moved to help him. Within a minute or so, Bill's foot was freed, but in the process of the two boys' tugging and pulling at the rocks, two fairly large rocks were dislodged from the creek bed. One of them seemed to pop to the surface, where it hit Billy in the head. Billy collapsed back into the water and his body began to tumble out of control downstream, caught in the swift current of that part of the creek. He struck his head on several other rocks as he was swept unconscious down the creek, with Roger screaming for help and scrambling alongside the creek bank as best he could. By the time George had moved upstream to the site of the accident, and he and Roger were eventually able to pull Bill's body from the creek, there was no sign of life.

The entire incident had happened in less than five minutes. Their lives, however, were changed forever.

What had been a happy, carefree, laughter-filled family outing turned into the darkest day of Paulette's life. The other children, Peter (only three at the time) and their twin daughters, Maggie and Maddie (age five), could not understand why their older brother Billy didn't move as he lay in their mother's arms in the back of the truck. George drove like a madman down the mountain to the hospital, hoping against hope that Billy might be revived by some miracle of medical science. Paulette held her young son's body, crying silently with a knowing deep in her heart that her son had left this world forever.

Now, Paulette was hearing Roger's frantic cry for help once again. She reached the well and discerned quickly that the wood cover over it had rotted through. It didn't take much for her to imagine Peter standing up on it to untangle the rope and bucket that hung above the well—he was probably trying to "help" by bringing in water to the kitchen. He probably had jumped up to reach the bucket and when he came down, the rotten boards broke under his weight. She quickly began to pull the rest of the boards away from the cover and to call into the well. There was no sound from the darkness below.

The doctor told her later that Peter never knew what had happened. The gashes on his head indicated that he had hit his head very hard on the boards and then on the stone side of the well as he fell to the water below. There had been no struggle once he hit the water. "Accidental death by drowning" was the coroner's ruling—the same wording he had used to describe the death of Billy three years before.

For days, Paulette sat in the big rocking chair in the living room, holding her baby son Eddie, who was only eight months old. She occasionally moved to help care for her toddler daughter Annie, now three. Over and over she thought, *Will I lose another child?* The dread and fear were almost overpowering at times.

At other times, she cried in grief—and guilt, "What kind of woman gives birth to seven children and loses two of them to drowning accidents?" Again and again, she replayed the two experiences in her mind, asking herself—even berating and blaming herself with—what-if questions: "What if I had insisted the boys not go upstream to fish?" "What if I had told them not to cross the creek?" "What if we had put a different cap on the well?" "What if I had not allowed Peter outside to 'play' that afternoon?" She even got so far as to question whether she had done the right thing in marrying a farmer instead of the city boy who had wanted to court her.

One day the pastor came to visit, and Paulette told him she didn't think she had been a good mother. The pastor reassured her repeatedly that she was one of the finest mothers he had ever known. When he couldn't seem to get through to her, he finally said, "Paulette, if you are determined to see yourself as a bad mother, let me ask you, what are you going to do about being a bad mother?"

"What can I do?" Paulette asked.

"Well, you could pray and ask God to forgive you for whatever it is that you think you might have done wrong in the past."

Paulette grinned and said, "That's what I need to do! Will you pray with me?" And right there in Paulette's living room, they prayed. Paulette got up out of that rocking chair and rarely returned to it for the next twenty years.

Only once did Paulette bring up these grievously sad incidents again, and that was the day she overheard two women talking in the church kitchen. They had no idea she was on the other side of the open door when one of them said something like this: "Not every child is part of the elect, of course. Just think about the Williams boys. God caused them to die when Billy was just seven and Peter was just six. They never had a chance to receive Jesus as their Savior."

"But do you think they went to hell?" the other woman asked.

"Where else would they go?" the first woman said.

Paulette was too stunned to enter the kitchen and confront the women. Instead she turned away, hurriedly scooped up her children, found George, and insisted they get home as quickly as possible. She found excuses to stay away from church for the next few Sundays.

Missing her, the pastor again drove out to their farm and when he asked Paulette why she hadn't been to church in three weeks, she sputtered out what she had overheard.

"Where do you think your boys are?" the pastor asked.

"They are in heaven with Jesus," Paulette said without a moment's hesitation. "I don't just think so. I know so." Pointing to her heart she added, "I know so right here."

The pastor said, "That's where I think your boys are too."

What the pastor didn't tell Paulette was that all the way back to town, he had a very tense conversation with God, asking God to show him that what he had said to Paulette was actually the truth. Where would God answer that prayer? As we have seen, in the Scripture. How many pastors have said what was "sentimentally necessary," only to later wonder if it was true? It was what the grieving mother wanted to hear, but was it what God wanted said? Thankfully, the servant of the Lord who intimately knows the Lord, and is indwelt by the Spirit of the Lord, is in touch with the compassion of the Lord—so what seems instinctively true is, in fact, in perfect harmony with God's Word.

Answers for the Questioning Heart

Paulette's experience points to a number of issues that are at the heart of why infants immediately find safety in the arms of God.

Some people divide infants into the chosen and nonchosen because they seek to affirm the clear and undeniable biblical doctrine of divine choice—that is, that God chooses who will be saved from sin and hell and live forever in heaven. The Bible clearly teaches that God chooses persons to salvation from eternity past, and that the salvation of those He chooses is by grace and grace alone. No one, therefore, who is saved in faith comes by any means other than God's choice according to His grace:

> Blessed be the God and Father of our Lord Jesus Christ, who has blessed us with every spiritual blessing in the heavenly places in Christ, just as He chose us in Him before the foundation of the world, that we should be holy and without blame before Him in love, having predestined us to adoption as sons by Jesus Christ to Himself, according to the good pleasure of His will, to the praise of the glory of His grace, by which He made us accepted in the Beloved. (Eph. 1:3–6)

Is there a biblical basis for believing that all persons who die in infancy are chosen for heaven by God? I believe there is.

I trust you to follow very closely and carefully the biblical evidence presented on the next few pages. Many people are quickly assured and temporarily comforted by the statement "Your baby is in heaven." Others are not. An explanation for *why* this is true is critical for them and, long-term, even for the superficially comforted. For all, I offer the following.

Biblical Truth #1: All children are conceived and born as sinners. If we truly are to deal with the issue of who is "elect" and who isn't, we must begin with the fact that all people are conceived and born as sinners. I know this is a difficult thing to face in a season of grief, but we cannot ignore it.

There is a widespread belief—even though it was condemned as heresy sixteen hundred years ago—that all people are born *without* sin. This view states that every soul is born as a morally clean slate, and sin takes root in a person's life only when he or she first engages in willful sin. Those who hold this belief contend that since a young child cannot make a willful choice to sin, the child who dies prior to sinning is an automatic candidate for heaven. In essence, a sinless child goes to a sinless eternity.

This belief was soundly condemned by every church council that met to consider the issue. The belief continues to survive today, however, in some circles.

The Bible states very clearly that all children are born as sinners from their conception. The principle of iniquity is embedded in the heart of every human being. Every person is born morally corrupt and born with an irresistible bent toward evil. Any notion that a child is born morally neutral, or that a baby is born without a predisposition to sin, is contrary to Scripture. When Scripture refers to infants as "innocent," it does not mean they are untainted by the fallenness or guilt we all inherit from Adam (Rom. 5:1–19).

If infants were not sinful or morally corrupt, they would not die at all! If babies were born totally without sin or depravity, there could be no reason for their death. The Bible says very clearly, "The wages of *sin* is death, but the gift of God is eternal life" (Rom. 6:23, emphasis added). Sin is the killer, the destroyer of life. The very fact that babies die at all bears evidence to the truth that sin is present in them—the disease of an inherited sin nature has within it the seeds of death.

Furthermore, do you know of any adult—apart from Jesus Christ—who ever chose *not* to sin at some point very early in his or her life? Such a person has never walked on this earth! Everyone has an automatic propensity or "bent" toward rebelling against God the very same way Adam and Eve rebelled against Him. The spirit of rebellion resides in every human heart—more blatantly and overtly in some, more subtly in others, but resident in all nonetheless.

Any child who lives to the point of making a responsible moral choice *will* make the choice to sin. It is in his or her nature.

Numerous passages in the Bible underscore this truth:

- They sin against You (for there is no one who does not sin). (1 Kings 8:46)
- Behold, I was brought forth in iniquity, and in sin my mother conceived me. (Ps. 51:5)
- The wicked are estranged from the womb; they go astray as soon as they are born, speaking lies. (Ps. 58:3)
- In Your sight no one living is righteous. (Ps. 143:2)
- Who can say, "I have made my heart clean, I am pure from my sin"? (Prov. 20:9)
- For there is not a just man on earth who does good and does not sin. (Eccl. 7:20)

- The heart is deceitful above all things, and desperately wicked; who can know it? (Jer. 17:9)

- There is none righteous, no, not one; there is none who understands; there is none who seeks after God. They have all turned aside; they have together become unprofitable; there is none who does good, no not one. (Rom. 3:10–12)

- We all once . . . were by nature children of wrath. (Eph. 2:3)

- You . . . were called a transgressor from the womb. (Isa. 48:8)

- The imagination of man's heart is evil from his youth. (Gen. 8:21)

The Scriptures cry out about the sinfulness of mankind! The Bible clearly states that we are "brought forth in iniquity" (Ps. 51:5). Thus, we all bear the stain of original sin. We are sinners from birth.

When David wrote, "In sin my mother conceived me," that is what he meant. He was not suggesting there was anything sinful about childbirth itself. Neither is sin embedded within a child based upon the physical or sexual facts surrounding that child's conception. Both parents may have been blatant sinners, and they may have sinned in having a sexual relationship that resulted in a conception, but that is not the sin that taints the child. If that were so, then those children born to righteous, married parents would be sinless—and that is not at all the case. Rather, the Bible declares that we all are sinners from conception and from birth because it is our *nature* as human beings to be sinners. Our sin nature is the result of the Fall in the Garden of Eden. We are inheritors of the sin nature acquired by our first ancestors, Adam and Eve.

Sinfulness is not a condition that comes upon people when they are old enough to make choices and decisions for themselves. It is a condition that is present in every human being from before birth. It is what produces our sinful choices. Every conception brings into being a sinful life. Every person born since Adam and Eve arrives on this earth in a sinful state. The apostle Paul wrote, "By one man's disobedience many were made sinners" (Rom. 5:19).

Because we are born as sinners, we each need to be "born again" if we are to experience a newness in our spiritual nature. Paul also wrote, "As sin reigned in death, even so grace might reign through righteousness to eternal life through Jesus Christ our Lord" (Rom. 5:21). If we were not born as sinners, we would not need salvation. The truth, however, is that "all have sinned and fall short of the glory of God," and all are therefore in need of "being justified freely by His grace through the redemption that is in Christ Jesus" (Rom. 3:23–24).

Every child is conceived bearing a deadly "sin" virus. He is born with corrupt motives, ambitions, attitudes, desires, and objectives latent in his heart.

So we cannot say that babies who die go to heaven because they are "sinless." Rather, babies who die go to heaven because God is gracious.

Biblical Truth #2: The salvation of every person is a matter of God's grace, not man's works. It is not an easy thing to think of babies as sinners, but it is true. The good news, however, is that babies who die are saved. And they are saved by the only means that anyone is saved: *God's grace*.

Let me point out to you that there are a number of church leaders who hold out that human beings must *do* certain things to ensure the salvation of babies. None of these positions is in line with the truth of God's Word. I'm going to briefly address them because you, as a grieving parent or family member, may encounter them.

Some in the history of the church have held to the position that infants will have an opportunity to come to Christ *after death*. This position is actually growing among many contemporary theologians, who claim that all people, regardless of their age at death, will have an after-death opportunity to confess Christ as Savior. While this may seem like a comforting thought to some, the problem with that position is, there is absolutely no basis in Scripture for believing such a thing. According to Hebrews 9:27, "It is appointed for men to die once, but after this the judgment." The idea of a second chance after death is a figment of someone's imagination, like the medieval idea that babies who died came back as fireflies.

Others contend that babies are saved if they are *baptized*. Those who hold this opinion believe God extends grace to babies, but only to *baptized* babies. One denomination's catechism says this about infant baptism: "Baptism worketh forgiveness of sins, delivers from death and the devil, and gives everlasting salvation to all who believe as the Word of the promise of God declares."

One of the early church teachers believed baptized infants went to heaven, while unbaptized infants did not, although he did declare that unbaptized infants receive immunity from the *pains* of hell. The truth is: Baptism cannot save any person. It is an ordinance clearly presented in the Scriptures as an act of obedient testimony for those who willfully believe the gospel—impossible for infants to do.

The Lutheran Augsburg Confession says about baptism: "Lutherans teach that it [baptism] is necessary to salvation, and that by baptism, the grace of God is offered, and that children are to be baptized, who by baptism being offered to God are received into God's favor." This view is held by Roman Catholics, Anglicans, Episcopalians, and some Reformed groups. The Council of Trent in 1563 based the salvation of infants upon Roman Catholic baptism. In 1951, Pope Pius XII taught that "no other way besides baptism is seen as imparting the life of Christ to little children." The new Roman Catholic catechism teaches that "by Christian baptism one enters into the kingdom of God and into the sphere of the saving work of Christ."

The fact is, there is no example of infant baptism in Scripture and, therefore, no comment on what it might accomplish. Still, to many, baptized babies are saved and unbaptized babies are not.

This, of course, makes salvation an act of "works"—the work

of baptism—not grace. There is no credit to the grace of God in such a view. Nor, according to those who hold the view, can any means of salvation be extended to the soul of an unborn child who is miscarried or aborted.

Others claim that because all babies are born sinful by nature, and they have no opportunity to believe in Jesus Christ, to repent, or to cry out to God for mercy, they are all damned to hell. I have heard this argument with increasing frequency in recent years.

The logic behind the argument is this: All babies are sinful, all sinners deserve hell; therefore, all babies who die in their sinful state go to hell.

People once accused the famous Calvinist theologian and preacher Charles Spurgeon of embracing a theology that damned infants to hell. Spurgeon responded by saying:

Among the gross falsehoods which have been uttered against the Calvinist proper is the wicked calumny that we hold *the damnation of little infants*. A baser lie was never uttered. There may have existed somewhere in some corner of the earth a miscreant who would dare to say that there were infants in hell, but I have never met with him, nor have I met with a man who ever saw such a person.

We say with regard to infants, Scripture saith but very little, and therefore where Scripture is confessedly scant, it is for no man to determine dogmatically. But I think I speak for the entire body, or certainly with exceedingly few exceptions, and those unknown to me, when I say, we hold that all infants [who die] are elect of God and are therefore saved, and we look to this as being the means by which Christ shall see of the travail of His soul to a great degree, and we do sometimes hope that thus the multitude of the saved shall be made to exceed the multitude of the *lost*.

Whatever views our friends may hold upon the point, they are not necessarily connected with Calvinistic doctrine. I believe that the Lord Jesus, who said "of such is the kingdom of heaven," doth daily and constantly receive into His loving arms those tender ones who are only shown and then snatched away to heaven.[1]

If you survey Reformed literature from the last four hundred years since Calvin, you will find that the vast majority of writers contend that infants who die are taken to heaven.

You may say, "Well, if God allows all babies into heaven, that's just grace."

Right!

Fallen, sinful, guilty and depraved children who die with no spiritual merit—no personal, moral, or religious merit—are welcomed by God into glory. On what basis? Solely by God's *grace*!

How were you or any other person saved? By law? Or by grace? None of us had any more to do with regard to the accomplishment of our own salvation than the youngest and most helpless infant. We all have been saved by *grace*.

Jesus said, "Unless you are converted and become as little

children, you will by no means enter the kingdom of heaven" (Matt. 18:3). None of us are capable of saving our own souls. We each must come as a little child—totally dependent upon God's grace—if we are to receive the free gift of mercy and forgiveness made possible by the death of Jesus Christ.

The apostle Paul said very clearly, "For by grace you have been saved through faith, and that not of yourselves; it is the gift of God, not of works, lest anyone should boast" (Eph. 2:8–9).

The salvation of every person is initiated by God and is His sovereign choice, through grace, based upon no merit whatsoever in the individual sinner. None of us deserves salvation—which means there is nothing we can do to earn, win, achieve, or otherwise attain salvation based upon our own merit, intelligence, good works, rational intellectual argument, religious or denominational affiliation, or family heritage. We can do nothing by any means to save ourselves. Salvation has nothing to do with our initiative or accomplishment. Salvation is all by grace. There is no clearer manifestation of this truth than the gift of eternal life given to a helpless, lost infant. The saving grace given to an infant who has no part whatsoever in his salvation is a perfect example of salvation, which is always wrought sovereignly by God through grace.

Biblical Truth #3: We are saved by the sacrificial work of Jesus Christ on the cross—the supreme manifestation of God's grace. The questions naturally arise: If infants are saved when they die, by what *means* are they saved? If adults are saved who are mentally disabled—those who are infants when it comes to understanding matters related to salvation—by what means are they saved?

The answer: by the sacrificial work of Jesus Christ. Our salvation is established by God's election of sinners to salvation *through Christ*. Scripture teaches that Jesus Christ is the sole and sufficient Savior. Salvation comes only on the basis of His blood atonement.

God has chosen those who will be saved, including those who die in infancy. They are saved not on their own initiative, but by His sovereign choice, through grace alone. Infants have no merit by which anyone could ever claim they *deserve* heaven. In fact, because of their guilt and corruption, they are in need of redemption, but their salvation is paid for by the substitutionary sacrifice of Christ on the cross, in which He bore the wrath of God not only for all who could believe, but also for those who could *not* believe.

B. B. Warfield, the definitive and revered Princeton theologian, once wrote:

The destiny of infants who die is determined irrespective of their choice, by an unconditional decree of God, suspended for its execution on no act of their own. And their salvation is wrought by an unconditional application of the grace of Christ to their souls, through the immediate and irresistible operation of the Holy Spirit prior to and apart from any action of their own proper wills. And if death in infancy does

depend on God's providence, it is assuredly God in His providence who selects this vast multitude to be made partici-
pants of His unconditional salvation. This is but to say that
they are unconditionally predestined to salvation from the
foundation of the world.[2]

If we understand that God by His nature is a Savior (see 1
Tim. 1:1; 4:10), is it not the truest expression of God's heart
that He chooses to save infants? How could we believe that
God weeps over the lost and pleads with *willful* sinners to be
reconciled to Him if He catapults millions upon millions of
innocent babies into hell before they even reach a state of
moral culpability—before they have the ability to make any
moral distinction between good and evil?

**Biblical Truth #4: We are saved by grace, but "damned" by
works.** It's important to ask, What *does* Scripture teach about
damnation? If a person is saved by grace, how is it that a person
is damned?

Revelation 20:11–15 describes the Great White Throne judgment seat of God:

Then I saw a great white throne and Him who sat on it,
from whose face the earth and the heaven fled away. And
there was found no place for them. And I saw the dead,
small and great, standing before God, and books were
opened. And another book was opened, which is the Book

of Life. And the dead were judged according to their works, by the things which were written in the books. The sea gave up the dead who were in it, and Death and Hades delivered up the dead who were in them. And they were judged, each one according to his works. Then Death and Hades were cast into the lake of fire. This is the second death. And anyone not found written in the Book of Life was cast into the lake of fire.

Scripture teaches that we are *saved* by grace, but we are *damned* by works. Scripture teaches that eternal punishment is the wage due those who have willfully sinned. Nowhere in the Bible is anyone ever threatened with hell merely for the guilt inherited from Adam. Instead, whenever Scripture describes the inhabitants of hell, the stress is on their *willful* acts of sin and rebellion (1 Cor. 6:9–10; Gal. 5:19–21; Eph. 5:5; Col. 3:6; Rev. 21:8; 22:15). Scripture always connects eternal condemnation with works of unrighteousness—willful sin.

No Willful Rebellion or Unbelief. The foremost work of the sinner is unbelief. That is the primary damning work. The Bible tells us, "He who believes in the Son has everlasting life; and he who does not believe the Son shall not see life, but the wrath of God abides on him" (John 3:36).

Jesus made this point very clearly when He taught in the temple, "I am going away, and you will seek Me, and will die in your sin. Where I go you cannot come." The Jewish leaders present asked among themselves, "Will He kill Himself, because He says, 'Where I go you cannot come'?" Jesus, knowing their question, said back to them, "You are from beneath; I am from above. You are of this world; I am not of this world. Therefore I said to you that you will die in your sins; for *if you do not believe that I am He, you will die in your sins*." (John 8:21–24, emphasis added)

Throughout the history of the church, unbelief has been singled out as the primary damning sin. A person who doesn't believe doesn't obey. Unbelief always produces evil works. It is this record of unbelief and subsequent evil works that is revealed in the Great White Throne judgment; this record becomes the basis for eternal condemnation.

Little children have no such record. They have no basis on which to believe or not believe. They are incapable of discerning right from wrong, sin from righteousness, evil from goodness. Scripture is very clear on this truth. Little children have no record of unbelief or evil works, and therefore, there is no basis for their deserving an eternity apart from God. As innocents, they are graciously and sovereignly saved by God as part of the atoning work of Christ Jesus.

As mentioned previously, after the children of Israel rebelled against God in the wilderness, God sentenced that entire generation to die in the wilderness after forty years of wandering. The Lord said, "Not one of these men of this evil generation shall see that good land of which I swore to give to your fathers" (Deut. 1:35). But God exempted young children and infants from this decree, and He explained why He did so: "Moreover your little ones and your children, who you say will be victims, *who today have no knowledge of good and evil,* they shall go in there; to them I will give it, and they shall possess it" (Deut. 1:39, emphasis added).

This inability to know right from wrong was also the criterion for innocence in the story of Jonah. Also as discussed previously, when Jonah complained to God about His sparing Nineveh, the great enemy city of Israel, the Lord replied, "Should I not pity Nineveh, that great city, in which are more than one hundred and twenty thousand persons who cannot discern between their right hand and their left?" (Jonah 4:11). The Lord was referring to the sparing of 120,000 *children,* little ones incapable of knowing right from left, much less right from wrong.

God had great compassion on those incapable of understanding truth.

Little children are called innocent in Scripture for precisely this reason: They have no willful rebellion against God. They have no deeds of disbelief. While they may be conceived with a sinful nature, they have never had willful opportunity to exercise that nature with full understanding or deliberate rebellion. And therefore, they are innocent of any deeds of unbelief against a holy God.

When people say, These little ones aren't saved because they didn't believe, my response is this: They *couldn't* believe. They are incapable of making a conscious, willful, rational, intentional choice to believe.

No Suppression of Truth. We read in the New Testament: "For the wrath of God is revealed from heaven against all ungodliness and unrighteousness of men, who suppress the truth in unrighteousness" (Rom. 1:18).

Divine judgment comes upon those who *suppress the truth*—who turn away from and deny the power of the truth of God in their lives and pursue the lies of the devil. In suppressing the truth and pursuing lies, they yield to the temptations of the devil to do evil, which may take any number of forms of rebellion and disbelief.

The apostle Paul also wrote to the Romans: "Although they knew God, they did not glorify Him as God, nor were thankful, but became futile in their thoughts, and their foolish hearts were darkened" (Rom. 1:21).

This foundational chapter of Romans makes it very clear that God reveals Himself to all people in sufficient measure to make His power, His moral government, and something of His glory obvious—through conscience, and through the light of nature. No person has an acceptable excuse for failing to perceive and understand the invisible attributes of God. Sinful men and women, however, choose to turn away from God, who has revealed Himself to them. They do not glorify Him. They give Him no thanks or praise. They turn their thoughts inward, away from God, and when they do so, their hearts become darkened.

They think they are wise, but they are fools. They begin to worship the works of their own hands, and when that happens, God allows them to wallow in their sin and the lust of their hearts. God gives them over to worship the creature rather than the Creator.

No infant suppresses the truth. A young child has no ability to perceive what God has revealed and made manifest and then reject it. Young children are not "futile in their thoughts." They have no awareness of the things God has revealed and, therefore, they can neither cry out to God nor turn away from Him. This, as we have seen, is precisely what Jonah 4:11 and Deuteronomy 1:39 teach.

Paul writes that because people "did not like to retain God in their knowledge, God gave them over to a debased mind, to do those things which are not fitting." He goes on to list a number of sinful behaviors and attitudes, including being "haters of God." This certainly does not describe a young child, who has no ability as yet to manifest hate toward God. It is these who *know* they are going against the righteous judgment of God who are "deserving of death" (Rom. 1:28–32).

A young child is truly incapable of rebellion against God because rebellion against God is rooted in deliberate, willful hatred of God. Speaking through the prophet Isaiah, the Lord said, "Before the Child shall know to refuse the evil and choose the good, the land that you dread will be forsaken by both her kings" (Isa. 7:16). The Lord was referring to the state of young childhood, a time when a person is incapable of making a willful choice to rebel against God. There is no statement in the Scriptures that indicates divine judgment comes to those who never have a knowledge of right and wrong, or who never have the opportunity to choose whether they will love or hate God.

No understanding of sin's impact or consequences. Children may be self-centered and selfish. They may throw tantrums, cry in anger, steal cookies, bop their siblings on the head, or kick sand into the faces of their little friends on the playground. They may defy their parents, saying "No" when the appropriate response is an obedient "Yes." They may lie to cover their misdeeds.

Certainly we are correct in assessing that all these actions are wrong—yes, even sinful.

But the *child* cannot assess in his own heart that his actions violate God or that there is any such concept as sin against God and His holy law. He knows that he has done something Mom and Dad don't like because Mom and Dad tell him so! He has no understanding that his rebellion, lying, stealing, and so forth are in violation of God's law and that such actions have any form of eternal consequence. Young children are incapable of understanding God in this way. They could not grasp the gospel if they heard it. They haven't any capacity to receive Jesus as Savior—to repent and believe—or to refuse Him.

They are, therefore, innocent of knowing the full importance, impact, or consequences of their actions. Infants who die do not have anything written in the record of heaven against them because they have never committed any *conscious* deeds of rebellion and iniquity against God. Young children are not yet responsible moral agents—in other words, they are not yet culpable for their actions because they simply do not fully know what they are doing and the consequences associated with their behavior.

R. A. Webb addressed this very point when he wrote:

> If a dead infant were sent to hell on no other account than that of original sin, there would be a good reason to the Divine Mind for the judgment, because sin is a reality. But the child's mind would be a perfect blank as to the reason of its suffering. Under such circumstances, it would know suffering but it would have no understanding of the reason for its suffering. It could not tell itself why it was so awfully smitten, and consequently, the whole meaning and significance of its sufferings, being to it a conscious enigma, the very essence of the penalty would be absent and justice would be disappointed, cheated of its validation.[3]

No debased behavior. Scripture teaches that we are judged on the basis of our deeds willfully committed "in the body" (2 Cor. 5:10). The sin of Adam and the resulting guilt explain our inability to be reconciled to God without being saved, but the Bible does not teach that we will answer or be held accountable for Adam's sin. We will answer for our own sin. What about infants? Have those who died in infancy committed such sins in the body? No.

Jesus said, "Those things which proceed out of the mouth come from the heart, and they defile a man. For out of the heart proceed evil thoughts, murders, adulteries, fornications, thefts, false witness, blasphemies. These are the things which defile a man" (Matt. 15:18–20). A young child is incapable of committing these sinful deeds that defile the soul and are subject to God's punishment.

Phil Johnson, an elder at Grace Community Church, wrote in one of his lessons,

I met one fellow whose own child died in infancy, and he seemed to think there was something meritorious about believing his own child had gone to hell. Every chance he got, he brought up the issue and boasted about how he and his wife had come to grips with the fact that their child was simply not among the elect. I told him I thought he and his wife were in for a pleasant surprise when they get to glory. I recall that he said he was absolutely certain that if God elected that infant to salvation, He would have kept him alive long enough to bring him to faith. My reply was that he would have had just as much biblical warrant to conclude that if God had decided *not* to elect that child, He would have kept him on earth long enough for the child's heart to be hardened by sin, and for his rebellion against God to be manifest through deliberate actions. Because *whenever Scripture describes the inhabitants of hell, it always does so with lists of sins and abominations they have deliberately committed.* We might look at the biblical data and conclude that when God takes the life of a little one, it is actually an act of mercy keeping that child from being hardened by a life of exposure to evil and a life of deliberate rebellion against God. One's position on this issue says a lot about one's view of God and His grace.[4]

No Ability to Choose Salvation. I am well aware that Jesus said we are to "enter by the narrow gate; for wide is the gate and broad is the way that leads to destruction, and there are many who go in by it. Because narrow is the gate and difficult is the way which leads to life, and there are few who find it" (Matt. 7:13–14). I believe Jesus was referring, however, to those intellectually *capable* of seeking the narrow way and morally culpable for failing to do so. To be able to find a way, you need to be able to search for that way. The very young are not capable of doing this.

Paul wrote to the Romans, "For as by one man's disobedience many were made sinners, so also by one Man's obedience many will be made righteous" (Rom. 5:19). The "many" in that verse, I believe, includes the little ones. One way to explain the fact that "few" find the narrow way and yet "many" are made righteous is to acknowledge that vast numbers of unborn, newly born, and young children have populated heaven since the beginning of time. It is by the grace of God that these little ones stand before Him today, fully transformed from a human nature of sin to a redeemed nature of righteousness.

A Sovereign Work of Christ Jesus. Let me bring this to a summary point. There is no place in Scripture in which a person suffers the judgment of damnation on the basis of anything other than sinful deeds, including the sinful *deed* of disbelief—a conscious, willful, intentional choice to disbelieve. Furthermore, God does not charge people with sins until sins are committed.

Salvation is completely by grace, apart from works. Damnation is completely by works, apart from grace.

In no place does Scripture teach infant damnation. Rather, every biblical reference—whether oblique or direct—to the issue of infants and children who die gives us reason to believe they go immediately into the eternal presence of God.

I cannot help but conclude that our Lord graciously and freely receives all those who die in infancy—not on the basis of their innocence or their worthiness, but by His grace, made theirs through the atonement He purchased on the cross. These little ones experience salvation grounded in absolute sovereignty and comprehensive grace.

Yes, children are sinners by nature. Babies are not without a sin nature—they are, however, without sin *deeds*.

Yes, children are in need of a Savior.

Yes, God has provided a Savior for them, Jesus Christ.

Yes, all children who die before they reach a state of moral awareness and culpability in which they understand their sin and corruption—so that their sins are deliberate—are graciously saved eternally by God through the work of Jesus Christ. They are counted as elect by sovereign choice because they are innocent of willful sin, rebellion, and unbelief, by which works they would be justly condemned to eternal punishment.

If you have followed thoughtfully all the Scripture in this and the previous chapter, you know your child who died prior to birth, at birth, or as a child too young to grasp the distinction between good and evil is indeed safe in the arms of God, eternally secure in His love and grace.

FIVE

Will I See My Child Again?

MOST PEOPLE WHO HAVE SOME FAMILIARITY WITH THE Bible know the story of David and Bathsheba. After committing adultery with Bathsheba, David discovered that she was pregnant with his child. He then sent Bathsheba's husband, Uriah, to the front lines of the hottest battle, a place where David knew with certainty Uriah would be killed. Before God, David was not only an adulterer, but also a murderer. The Lord sent His prophet Nathan to say as much to David (2 Sam. 11–12).

When confronted, David admitted what he had done. He said to Nathan, "I have sinned against the LORD" (2 Sam. 12:13). Nathan responded to David that the Lord had accepted his penitence and forgiven him—and therefore he would not die. He then stated that because what David had done had given great occasion for the Israelites' enemies to blaspheme against God, the child that Bathsheba had conceived would surely die (2 Sam. 12:14).

In essence, David was forgiven his sin, but the consequences of his sin were not going to be completely obliterated.

When Bathsheba's child was born, the infant was extremely sick. David pleaded with God for the life of the baby. He fasted and prayed, and we read that he "lay all night on the ground" as he begged God to save their baby boy. The servants of his household tried to get David to rise up and eat, but he wouldn't do either. He continued to fast and pray without ceasing, remaining in a prostrate position before the Lord. I'm sure David felt that the child's survival would represent God's mercy on him after his horrible iniquities. At least there would be one thing to alleviate the guilt—a new little son.

The baby died on the seventh day.

Having seen David suffer so profoundly and deeply over the illness of this child, the servants were afraid to tell David that the child had died. They were afraid David might kill himself upon hearing the news! They could see that David had attached all his personal sense of guilt, shame, and general well-being to the survival of this illegitimate son.

When David heard his servants whispering, he perceived the child was dead. He asked, "Is the child dead?" And they said, "He is dead."

Startlingly, it was at that point David arose from the ground, washed and anointed himself, changed clothes, and then went to the house of the Lord to worship. Afterward, he returned to his house. He requested that food be set before him and he ate. All the intense intercession, fasting, sorrow, and suffering was over—that fast.

David's servants were astonished. They had seen how distraught

David was at the illness and impending death of his son. They were so concerned about him that they guarded him carefully lest he try to do himself harm in a state of intense grief. Yet instead of seeing greater mourning from David, they saw their master clean up, worship God, and ask for something to eat. They couldn't help but question his behavior, asking him, "What is this that you have done? You fasted and wept for the child while he was alive, but when the child died, you arose and ate food" (2 Sam. 12:21).

David replied, "While the child was alive, I fasted and wept; for I said, 'Who can tell whether the LORD will be gracious to me, that the child may live?' But now he is dead; why should I fast? Can I bring him back again? I shall go to him, but he shall not return to me" (vv. 22–23).

David cherished this little child. Even though he knew his son had been conceived in sin, he loved him and wanted him to live. He fasted and prayed intensely for his fragile life. Like us, David had strong hopes that the Lord would graciously relent and allow the child to live—but he had no assurance that God would do so.

Here's the key to the change in David. He ceased his mourning after the baby died. He felt no further reason to fast and pray because his sorrow was instantly and completely replaced by hope. He declared, "I shall go to him, but he shall not return to me" (v. 23).

In spite of his sins, David was a man of God, and his theology was sound. He was a believer. He was chastened. And he was forgiven. He was God's child. So we know that David certainly wasn't referring to hell when he said, "I shall go to him."

There are those who say, "Well, what David meant was that they'd lie together in the same burial place in the field." How absurd! That idea certainly isn't going to make a person want to clean up and have a meal.

There are also those who say, "That child was going to hell because he was a child born of adultery." Scripture gives absolutely no support to that belief. As you will recall, the exact opposite is what Scripture supports:

The soul who sins shall die. The son shall not bear the guilt of the father, nor the father bear the guilt of the son. The righteousness of the righteous shall be upon himself, and the wickedness of the wicked shall be upon himself. (Ezek. 18:20)

David was able to say, "I shall go to him," because David knew where both he and his infant son were going! He knew that their eternal future was with God. This was the man who wrote, "Surely goodness and mercy shall follow me all the days of my life; and I will dwell in the house of the LORD forever" (Ps. 23:6).

And it was David who said, "As for me, I will see Your face in righteousness; I shall be satisfied when I awake in your likeness" (Ps. 17:15).

In Psalm 16, David wrote, "My heart is glad, and my glory rejoices; my flesh also will rest in hope. For You will not leave my soul in Sheol, nor will You allow Your Holy One to see corruption.

You will show me the path of life; in Your presence is fullness of joy; at Your right hand are pleasures forevermore" (vv. 9–11).

David *knew* that at his death he would be going into the near presence of the Lord, and he also knew that this was the eternal home for his baby.

A Story with a Different Ending

The baby born to Bathsheba was not David's only son. He had other sons including Absalom, who was an adult at the time of this baby's birth. Absalom later turned against his father and led a political revolt against him, cursing his father as he drove him from the throne in Jerusalem. He was not content to force David from the city, but he pursued him with the intent of killing him.

While Absalom was in pursuit of his father, he failed to duck as he rode his mule through a forest, and his head became stuck in the thick boughs of a terebinth tree. He was left dangling there, unable to free himself and unable to touch the ground (2 Sam. 18). When word came to Joab, one of David's generals, Joab immediately went to the scene, took three spears and thrust them through the heart of Absalom's dangling body, and then ten other young soldiers who were Joab's armor bearers surrounded Absalom and struck him. They cut down Absalom's dead body from the tree, dug a large pit in the woods, and buried the corpse right there. They then covered the grave with stones.

When a Cushite messenger came to David from the battle-front, he asked him, "Is the young man Absalom safe?" The messenger replied, "May the enemies of my lord the king, and all who rise against you to do harm, be like that young man!" The king knew immediately that his son was dead. The Bible tells us, "Then the king was deeply moved, and went up to the chamber over the gate, and wept. And as he went, he said thus: 'O my son Absalom—my son, my son Absalom—if only I had died in your place! O Absalom my son, my son!'" (2 Sam. 18:32–33).

David wept uncontrollably and mourned inconsolably for Absalom. What would otherwise have been a day of victory against a deadly enemy became a day of immense and agonizing mourning. Word quickly spread: "The king is grieved for his son" (2 Sam. 19:2). David covered his face and continued to cry out as the people returned to the city, "O my son Absalom! O Absalom, my son, my son!" (19:4).

What a contrast from David's response to the death of his infant son born to Bathsheba. David *stopped* mourning when his and Bathsheba's baby died; he *started* mourning when Absalom died. What was the difference? David knew that the baby was with the Lord, residing in the heavenly presence forever. He knew that Absalom—his wicked and rebellious adult son—was not. David could anticipate with hope a reunion with his infant son. He had no hope of ever seeing the wicked Absalom again.

David mourned for Absalom with unrelieved grief, just as any parent would do over a child who had rebelled against God and died in his sin without repentance.

Shall We Mourn or Rejoice?

I believe the following lessons can be drawn from these incidents in the life of King David:

- If you have a little one who dies, rather than focus on your human loss, look to the eternal gain of your child. Your child has attained eternal glory. Your little one is safely in the arms of God, alive forever and fully mature and like Christ.

- Especially for those who die in the womb, at birth, or in very young stages of infancy—rejoice that your child has not known the wickedness of this world. Your child has not struggled against temptation or been subject to the inner pull of sin's desires.

- Your young child who has died did not lose his or her life, but rather, your child has gained eternal life.

Focus Loving Concern on Your Living Children

Even as you rejoice on behalf of an infant who is with the Lord, be concerned for those children who live and who have not yet believed and received the saving grace of Jesus Christ.

Our tears need to be directed to those who are not following Jesus Christ as their Lord. Focus your prayers and shower your love on your children who are old enough to receive or reject the gospel. Take up the opportunity and responsibility you have to present the love and mercy of Christ Jesus to them in a convincing way. Urge them to repent of their sins and embrace the salvation in Christ alone. Beseech them to be reconciled to God (2 Cor. 5:20).

It is before our living children that we must do our utmost to set an example. We are commanded to do all we can to bring them up in the nurture and admonition of the Lord, to surround them with godly influence and present to them the truth of the gospel, and to pray for them without ceasing. Our challenge is to help those children who survive the womb, infancy, and their young childhood to be ready to enter eternity on the day when God also calls them home.

Examine Your Own Heart

How would you personally answer the question "Will I see my child again?" The answer depends on your own believing and receiving of Jesus Christ as your Savior. Your joy in anticipating a reunion with your little one who died is dependent on your knowing you are going to the place where he or she is. David had that confidence. Do you?

Nothing in Scripture suggests that children in eternity are aware of their parents' lives on this earth, or that those children influence what happens to their parents. To hope that in some way a child's safety in the arms of God might result in the salvation of a parent is a false hope.

Your child will greet you in eternity one day *only* if you have believed in and received Christ Jesus as your personal Savior. The gospel calls you to repent of your sins and place your faith in Christ as the only Savior. You have no hope of joining your child in heaven unless you have responded to Christ in faith.

A question may arise in the hearts of some who have committed grievous sins that were related to the death of their child: "Can God forgive me for what I have done? Can God forgive me for the way in which I failed my child?" These questions seem to haunt many parents whose children died as a result of their neglect, failure, abuse, or willful seeking of an abortion.

If you have asked such questions, I have good news. Scripture promises full and free forgiveness to all who seek mercy through Christ:

- "Come now, and let us reason together," says the LORD, "though your sins are like scarlet, they shall be as white as snow; though they are red like crimson, they shall be as wool." (Isa. 1:18)

- Let the wicked forsake his way, and the unrighteous man his thoughts; let him return to the LORD, and He will have mercy on him; and to our God, for He will abundantly pardon. (Isa. 55:7)

- This is a faithful saying and worthy of all acceptance, that Christ Jesus came into the world to save sinners, of whom I am chief. (1 Tim. 1:15)

Let me share one woman's poignant story with you.

Julene was only twenty years old when she had an abortion. She had no regrets about her action—at the time of the abortion, that is. She had been studying overseas on a "junior year abroad program" when she fell in love with another student who had come to this foreign university from yet another nation. She and her boyfriend had been sharing an apartment for two months when she discovered she was pregnant.

The very day Julene learned she was pregnant, she made the decision to have an abortion. She never told her boyfriend about her decision until after the procedure was over. She simply went to a clinic recommended by a friend and, brushing aside all counseling offered to her there, she scheduled the procedure for the very next day. As you might have anticipated, Julene and her boyfriend ended their relationship shortly after he learned what had happened, and each went back to their respective countries two months later and never had contact again. For Julene's part, she returned home feeling incredibly older, wiser, and yet strangely more sad, depressed, and uneasy than ever in her life.

Even in her sadness, Julene tried to convince herself that there had really been no other option. She could not imagine having told her parents that she was pregnant, or for that matter, that she had a boyfriend with whom she had entered into a sexual relationship. Julene had been raised in a Christian home, and she knew that her parents fully believed their daughter had remained faithful to all they expected of her during her overseas term of study—they had no idea she had sinned or to what extent—and Julene couldn't bring herself to tell them.

She also tried to convince herself that the fetus she had aborted was just that—a "fetus." She would not allow herself to use the word *baby*. She tried to convince herself that there was absolutely no way she could have raised a baby on her own or even with the help of friends. After all, she had a year of college to complete, a career to forge, a future husband to meet. She chalked up her entire romantic relationship, sexual liaison, and abortion as a "bad experience." She tried to place blame on the loneliness she had felt overseas, the overtly sexual messages that seemed to permeate the campus where she had gone to study, and the overpowering "chemistry" she had felt for the young man whom she had allowed to seduce her. She tried to convince herself that she had done what any rational twenty-year-old girl in her situation would have done, and that she had acted responsibly and as an adult.

Yes, she tried and tried to convince herself of these positions, but deep inside, Julene remained troubled. She lost considerable weight, but rather than be alarmed at this, Julene was excited that she was thinner than she had been when she went overseas, and her parents and others gave her compliments on the "sleek new woman" they saw before them as a college senior. And then, on the very day in October that she had initially been told would be the due date for her baby, Julene had a serious breakdown. She was at home visiting her parents for the weekend, saw a young couple out on the sidewalk with their baby in a stroller, and without any warning, emotions deep within her heart welled up and she began to sob uncontrollably. She could hardly be consoled. When her mother finally was able to hold her to the point of her becoming quiet in her arms, her mother asked, "Are you sick, honey?"

Julene replied that she hadn't felt like herself for several months, as if she was fighting an infection of some type. The next day, Julene and her mother went to their family physician. Within a matter of days, Julene learned that yes, indeed, she was fighting an infection, which had begun at the time of the abortion. Furthermore, she learned that since the infection had gone so long untreated, there was a strong likelihood that she would *not* be able to conceive or bear a child in the future. The procedure performed on her body in that foreign land had not gone nearly as well as Julene had thought—in truth, she had been mangled by the process. Over the next few days, Julene shared the full truth of her pregnancy and abortion with her parents, underwent a D&C at the local hospital, and began a course of antibacterial therapy.

To Julene's surprise, her parents were remarkably and genuinely understanding and forgiving—once they got beyond their initial shock, of course. They embraced their daughter with love and invited Julene to move home, where her mother began to cook nutritional meals for her and care for her to help her regain her strength. Julene was grateful for their support since it was all she could do to attend classes and study for exams. She struggled valiantly to complete the fall semester with passing grades.

By the next semester, Julene had recovered much of her physical strength and her emotional well-being. She had resisted returning to church after the truth came out about her pregnancy and abortion, and her parents didn't press the matter, but about Easter time, she began attending church again. She admitted to her mother, "I can't stop thinking that I murdered my baby. I seemed to be fine when I thought of having just a 'fetus' in me, but when I saw that couple out with their baby for a walk, I suddenly became overwhelmed by the idea that I had been pregnant with a *baby*. It was the first time after having the abortion that I really cried all the way to my toes." Mourning and seeking God's forgiveness began her healing.

Julene has been forgiven by God, and she can rejoice that she will be reunited with her child one day in heaven. She has hope today—not despair. She has a freedom to love and serve God fully—she knows she is forgiven. She enjoys thinking about her child, loving her child, and anticipating the day she will meet her child—rather than feeling fear and dread.

Can God forgive a person who kills a child, even his or her own flesh and blood? Yes. God's grace covers all magnitudes of sin.

If you believe you are responsible in any way for the death of your child, the question is not "Can God forgive?" but rather, "Will you receive God's forgiveness?" Will you accept God's freely offered mercy and grace in Jesus Christ? Will you be reconciled with God (2 Cor. 5:20)?

And then, having embraced God's forgiveness, will you move forward in your life, intent on obedience to His commandments and with a commitment to sin no more (John 8:11)? These are the challenges a parent faces in the aftermath of a baby's death in which the parent believes he or she has some fault.

Will you see your child again?

If you receive Jesus as your Savior and experience His forgiveness of your sin, yes, you will.

Your child's death and the salvation of your children. The death of a child has profound impact on other siblings in a family—not only those who are alive at the time the child dies, but those born after the child's death. In many ways, the death of a child can be a catalyst for a sibling to come to know the Lord.

I recently heard the story of a woman named Sandra. Her story encapsulates much of the truth we've already covered in this book, so I am going to share it with you in its entirety. The ending of her story, however, is one I find extremely encouraging!

Sandra was in the sixth month of her pregnancy when, without warning, the placenta of her womb ripped and in less than an hour, she found herself in an emergency room and without child. The physicians and nurses who attended her tried to encourage her that it was almost a miracle she had not experienced further complications in this miscarriage. Her husband, who had rushed to her side from his place of employment the minute he heard she was on her way to the hospital, consoled her as well as he could. Her sister cried with her.

"But then," Sandra said later to her pastor, "when I left the hospital, everybody assumed that everything would be all right. They all seemed to have a that-was-then, this-is-now attitude. Nobody—not even my sister or husband—wanted to talk about the pregnancy. They all acted as if the baby I had been carrying wasn't a person—wasn't a life—because it had never been born.

"They didn't seem to understand that this baby girl was in every way a person to me. I sang to her and talked to her all my waking hours. I felt her kick within me. I had named her Rosemaree.

"It didn't matter that I had three healthy children when I became pregnant with Rosemaree. People kept saying to me, 'You have such a wonderful family'—as if trying to convince me that God had said, 'Enough is enough.' They didn't seem to understand that I wanted this little girl as much as I had wanted my other three children. She was not an accident. She was planned, desired, and very much 'expected' as a baby and as a part of our family."

Sandra had sought out her pastor because she still found herself mourning the loss of her unborn child four months after her miscarriage. She had a deep sorrow and a lingering listlessness that she could not shake. Her physician had pronounced her healthy and told her she would very likely be able to conceive again if she so desired. Sandra had not been interested in hearing that news—she was too filled with sadness over the absence of the newborn baby from her arms. Finally, her physician recommended medication to Sandra to help her with depression. It was at that point that Sandra sought out a member of the pastoral counseling staff at her church.

Fortunately, Sandra confided her story to a pastor who understood that Sandra's baby was in heaven, very much a person, worshiping God and enjoying the perfection of an eternal life in His presence. He mourned the loss of Rosemaree with Sandra, and the two of them planned a very simple prayer service to which Sandra invited her husband, sister, and other children. Even though the youngest of the siblings was only two, Sandra felt he needed to be part of the family circle as they met to praise God that their sister Rosemaree was in heaven. The service was held the following week in the quiet of a small church chapel on a Sunday afternoon.

Sandra later said, "That very simple service, which probably didn't last more than fifteen minutes, brought tremendous peace to my heart. My husband and sister had a new appreciation for the way I had felt about our unborn child. And for me, the service marked the true end of my grieving. From that afternoon on, I had a different perspective and a renewed joy in my life. I felt like moving forward in a way I can't fully explain. It was as if Rosemaree needed to be 'acknowledged' in a formal, spiritual way so I could fully entrust her to heaven and continue to live my life on this earth."

The next year, Sandra was pregnant again. This time, the pregnancy came to full term and she gave birth to a healthy baby boy. Two years later, another daughter was born to Sandra and her husband, Cliff.

Sandra said not long ago, "Someone noted just recently that our children are stairsteps in their ages—thirteen, eleven, nine, and then a skip to five and three. I said, 'Yes, we seemed to have a child every two years like clockwork—all their birthdays are in March and April! The child who would have been seven right now is Rosemaree. She is in heaven.'"

Sandra is right to say, "I have six children. Five on this earth and one already safely in the arms of God." One of the miracles that has come from Rosemaree's life happened just recently. As she explains, "Our oldest child, Stacie, came to us just a few months ago and said, 'Mom and Dad, I need to tell you what happened to me at church camp. I gave my life to the Lord during a prayer service one evening and I know I'm born again and am going to spend eternity with Jesus in heaven. The preacher at the camp said that if we had trusted Jesus for salvation we needed to tell our parents.'

"We rejoiced with Stacie, as you can imagine, and we were elated as parents that she had made this very adult step to a full commitment of her life to Christ. We were surprised, however, when she said, 'One of the things I got to thinking about was Rosemaree. I thought, *If I'm ever going to meet my little sister Rosemaree, I've got to confess Jesus as Lord and Savior and live for Him because Rosemaree is already in heaven and is living for Him in every way.*' My heart nearly burst. I didn't know whether Stacie even remembered Rosemaree. Later, Stacie told her brothers Max and Joey about her decision. To our surprise, Max also remembered the service we had held for Rosemaree. Both boys began asking questions about their 'sister in heaven.' In a strange way, Rosemaree has set the standard for her siblings. She is with the Lord, fully serving Jesus—and the challenge that lies before them is to believe in the Lord Jesus so that they will also be with the Lord and with her. Rosemaree is something of an unseen evangelist to our other children. I praise God for that!"

Will your children see their brother or sister again in heaven? It's a great question to ask them!

SIX

What Is My Child's Life Like in Heaven?

ONE OF THE GREAT TRAGEDIES OF OUR TIME HAS COME to be called "sudden infant death syndrome" or SIDS. Although certain risk factors are known, nobody knows with certainty what causes SIDS or what might be done to ensure it will not strike a child. A couple in our church, Jonathan and Stephanie, know the tragedy of losing a child to SIDS. Jonathan wrote to me with great grace and strength several years after the tragic night their son died:

> Racing behind an ambulance that cool September night, the words of Romans 8:28 suddenly became very *real* to me. Terror had struck our hearts just minutes earlier when we found our three and a half month old baby boy, Stephen Paul, lying lifeless in his crib. After frantic phone calls and desperate CPR measures, our son was suddenly on his way to the emergency room in a blur of whirling lights and a wailing

siren. "And we know that all things work together for good to those who love God, to those who are the called according to His purpose." As we quoted that verse of Scripture to ourselves over and over, we had a calm assurance that whatever the outcome we faced, God meant this for our good. We believed with all our hearts that God's power would revive our son. We believed that the Lord sovereignly stood watch over us. Our faith was strengthened.

After what seemed like an endless night, we were greeted the next morning by a host of Christian brothers and sisters—friends who began to minister to us faithfully and tirelessly. Our hopes had been dashed. Our son had died. And as we tried to come to grips with that reality, we found ourselves facing an even deeper reality—our son was in the presence of Christ and had begun his eternal life of worship before the Lord's throne. My first thoughts that next morning were from the hymn "My Hope Is in the Lord"—especially the line "For me He died, for me He lives, and everlasting light and life He freely gives." We comforted each other with this God-given hope that our son was not spared for us—and thus bound to a life of pain and sin—but was now safe with Him and eternally secure. Because we truly believed the words of Romans 8:28, we *knew* this tragic event was somehow for our good and God had *purposed it* for His glory.

After some investigation, our son's death was determined to be a case of sudden infant death syndrome. SIDS is still an "unexplainable event"—no concrete medical evidence exists to explain why he suddenly stopped breathing. Once we were labeled a SIDS case, literature began pouring in. We were offered group therapy meetings—an opportunity to meet with other parents in a similar situation—and we were given books and flyers outlining the medical explanations about what *may* have caused the death and how we *might* have avoided his death. Quite frankly, much of this literature left us hopeless and caused a significant amount of guilt and anguish. Our thoughts turned continually to the question "Could we have saved our son?" and we had many restless moments of doubt and fear. The psychological pamphlets were even worse for us than the medical explanations. Most of these offered an array of emotional strategies for getting through the grieving process. But because they failed to mention Jesus Christ, they left us feeling empty, as if this work of grieving was all on our shoulders.

Again and again, we felt as if Satan was using the world's attempts at comfort to assault God's promises instead. We are so thankful for our Christian friends, whose presence and prayers and words of true comfort reminded us that God is faithful and that God has a sovereign plan for our good—His purposes cannot be thwarted!

Our son died on September 22, 1998. When we reflect back on all the lessons the Lord taught us in the months that followed that dark day, we marvel at the way He carried us through that experience. We are so thankful for His mercy and grace. We are also ever grateful for the ministry of the church to us during that most desperate of times. I have never experienced the power of prayer, or felt Christ's presence so vividly before or since. God personally revealed Himself to us as our Refuge, Shelter, and the Shepherd of the Psalms. He was our daily Manna who alone could satisfy the emptiness we felt inside. We were able to identify with Abraham and his unwavering trust when God asked him to sacrifice his son.

Our son's death also raised in us our own anticipation of heaven. It unleashed our hold on the temporal things of this world. It transformed our understanding of God's sovereignty over *all* things. How we thank God for these works of God's grace in our lives!

We miss our son. Every day that passes reminds us of what he might have been, or what he could have done. Our disappointment in not sharing his life, however, is overshadowed by the promises of God's Word. Our son's grave marker quotes Jude 24–25, which I believe aptly sums up our perspective in dealing with the loss of Stephen Paul: "Now to Him who is able to keep you from stumbling, and to present you faultless with great joy, to Him alone be glory, dominion, and power both now and forever."

We have learned a number of life-lessons through our tragedy—lessons we would never have learned any other way. To become more like Christ has become our singular desire until the day of our reunion with our son in heaven. On that day we will fall down and worship the Lord together with him—forever. What a glorious hope that is!

What a glorious hope every parent should have after the death of a young child! The hope of heaven is truly *glorious* hope.

What Is Heaven Going to Be Like?

Through the years, many people have asked me what I believe heaven is going to be like. I tell them it's going to be just as the Bible describes it. One word describes our future life in heaven: *perfection*.

Most of us understand the general concept of perfection, but we have a very difficult time envisioning anything that is truly perfect. Everything in our earthly experience is flawed or imperfect in some way. All of creation is presently agonizing under the cruel effects of sin's curse, waiting for the consummation of all things when the curse is finally removed. At that time, everything will be perfect. Pain, sorrow, and the groaning of creation will end. We will know joy and gladness. Sorrow and sighing will be no more (Isa. 35:10; Rom. 8:22).

For our loved ones in heaven, including our little ones, that day of perfection has already come. They live as whole persons—whole in body and soul, completely new and flawless. The apostle John wrote, "Beloved, now we are the children of God; and it has not yet been revealed what we shall be, but we know that when He is revealed, we shall be like Him, for we shall see Him as He is" (1 John 3:2). Everything we can envision as the wholeness and perfection of Christ is the wholeness and perfection being experienced by our loved ones who dwell with Him in eternity.

The very moment your child saw Christ, your child was instantly and summarily made utterly perfect, completely transformed into the image of Christ Jesus.

Your child has a desire to please God—a heart for worship and praise and service to God.

Your child has a glory about him or her that cannot fade. It is a glory that comes from the inside out (Rom. 8:18).

One of the word pictures that is used in Scripture to describe those who dwell in heaven is the image of a white robe. Revelation 6:11 says, "A white robe was given to each of them." The white robe symbolizes holiness and purity and adorns each child in heaven.

Your child experiences none of what we know as human frailty or fallenness. The Lord has lovingly and graciously bestowed on your child—heart, soul, mind, and flesh—the standard befitting the lofty position He has elevated your child to occupy. He has given your child the standard of perfection so that he might stand before His throne and see God face-to-face.

There is no waiting period for this glorification. There is no "soul sleep" or purgatory. Nothing in Scripture even hints at such notions, and nothing indicates that our glorification after death will in any way be painful or require any after-death acts of repentance of our part. On the contrary, Christ Himself made full atonement for the sins of His people (2 Cor. 5:21; 1 Peter 2:24; 1 John 2:2). Salvation is a free and gracious gift of God. Every aspect of it, from our election in eternity past to our glorification in eternity future, is His work alone (Rom. 8:29–30). Scripture says that to depart this world is to be with Christ (Phil. 1:23). Upon seeing Christ, we become like Him. The transition is graceful, peaceful, painless, and instantaneous. The apostle Paul wrote, "To be absent from the body" is "to be present with the Lord" (2 Cor. 5:8).

What is the perfected soul like? The most obvious truth is that it will finally be perfectly free from evil forever. Your child will

- never have a selfish desire,
- never utter a useless word,
- never perform an unkind deed,
- never think a sinful thought.

Your child is completely liberated from any temptation to sin and is able to do all that is absolutely righteous and holy. Your child will experience

- no suffering,
- no sorrow,
- no pain.

Your child will never do anything displeasing to God. Because your child dwells in heaven where there is no taint of sin whatsoever, your child will live totally

- free of persecution,
- free of division,
- free of disunity,
- free of hate,
- free of quarrels or disagreements,
- free of disappointments.

Your child will not weep because there will be nothing to make your child sad. Your child will have no need to pray, fast, repent, or confess sin because there will be nothing to confess and nothing to pray for!

Your child will know a life of unimaginable blessing—and only blessing—for all eternity.

Perfect pleasure. Psalm 16:11 says, "In Your presence is fullness of joy; at Your right hand are pleasures forevermore." Everything that now gives us pure pleasure and genuine joy is multiplied beyond measure in heaven. And since nothing is better or greater than God, the pure enjoyment of being with the Father will be the very essence of the bliss your child enjoys.

Perfect knowledge. In heaven, your child lives in perfect knowledge—as complete a knowledge as your child could ever desire. Your child will never experience an unanswered question or an unsolved problem. Your child is living totally free of confusion and ignorance.

Perfect comfort. Your child will never experience even one uncomfortable moment. Heaven is a place of eternal comfort. Jesus, in telling the story of a beggar named Lazarus and a rich man, noted that in heaven Lazarus was "comforted," while the rich man was "in torments in Hades" (Luke 16:19–25).

Perfect love. Your child has a capacity to love perfectly and be loved perfectly. John 13:1 says Christ loved His disciples *eis telos*—which means "to the end, to utter perfection." That same love engulfs us forever in heaven. In heaven, your child is capable not only of receiving that love—in a way we cannot fully receive it on this earth—but also of expressing that love perfectly.

Perfect joy. Life on this earth is always mixed with a measure of sorrow, discouragement, disappointment, worry, struggle, and pain. Not so in heaven! Heaven is a place of undiluted joy. In the parable of the talents we find a recurring refrain: "Well done, good and faithful servant . . . Enter into the joy of your lord" (Matt. 25:21, 23). This is the message to all who enter the presence of the Lord in heaven—they are rewarded with the *fullness* of joy.

Perhaps best of all, these attributes of perfect pleasure, perfect knowledge, perfect comfort, perfect love, and perfect joy are *unending* and *never-diminishing* for your child. Heavenly perfection is never altered or diluted.

What Age Is My Child in Heaven?

Several parents have asked me this question. I have rephrased the question on occasion to ask, "Are there strollers in heaven?"

The answer is "No."

Whatever the child's imperfections, limitations, or immaturity here on earth, they are not present in heaven. In heaven, we will be conformed to Christ's image (Rom. 8:29). We will be like Jesus (1 John 3:2).

All the redeemed, of all ages and from all centuries, will be occupied doing one particular activity in heaven: "After these things I looked, and behold, a great multitude which no one could number, of all nations, tribes, peoples, and tongues, standing before the throne and before the Lamb, clothed with white robes, with palm branches in their hands, and crying out with a loud voice, saying, 'Salvation belongs to our God who sits on the throne, and to the Lamb!'" (Rev. 7:9–10).

The redeemed will join the angels and elders and living creatures as they fall on their faces before the throne of God and worship Him, saying:

> Amen! Blessing and glory and wisdom,
> Thanksgiving and honor and power and might,
> Be to our God forever and ever. Amen. (Rev. 7:12)

The largest number of this group may very well be the unborn and the young children saved through the ages by God's sovereign grace. They will come from every nation, tongue, tribe, and people. They are all capable of praising and worshiping God. They must possess, therefore, enough maturity to voice this praise and to understand the significance of their praise.

Other snapshots of heaven are given in the book of Revelation. In chapter 5 we read that "every creature which is in heaven and on the earth" stands before the Lord and says:

> Blessing and honor and glory and power
> Be to Him who sits on the throne,
> And to the Lamb, forever and ever! (Rev. 5:13)

At no point do we read in Scripture that there are those in heaven who are incapable of worship, incapable of voicing praise, or incapable of falling prostrate in their worship before the throne of God.

Will My Child Know Me?

Parents who have lost a child frequently ask, "Will my baby know me in heaven? Will I know my baby?"

Remember that King David said of his little son who died, "I shall go to *him*" (2 Sam. 12:23, emphasis added). He did not say, "I will go to his place," or "I will go to heaven where he is."

Heaven is a place of perfect reunions where we are known fully even as we know others fully. Scripture tells us, "Now we see in a mirror, dimly, but then face to face. Now I know in part, but then I shall know just as I also am known" (1 Cor. 13:12). In the same way the Lord knows you, you will know the Lord. In the same way the Lord knows you, you will also be known by others—and in like manner, you will know them.

Heaven is a place of perfect knowledge, perfect maturity, and perfect love.

What good news this is! A *person* whom you conceived is perfect, whole, and forever praising God. A *person* whom you conceived is before the throne of God. A *person* whom God created using the genetic material of you and your child's other parent is standing before the Lord in the *fullness* of his or her life. If you have accepted Jesus as your Savior, you will be united with that child one day, and *together,* you will praise the Lord through all eternity.

Your Child Will Have a Glorified Body

Heaven is not a "state of mind"—it is a real place where the redeemed have real bodies in the likeness of the body Jesus Christ had after the resurrection.

God made mankind with a body and soul, an inner and outer man (Gen. 2:7). Therefore, ultimate perfection demands that both body and soul be renewed.

Death results, of course, in separation of the body and soul. Our bodies go to the grave, and our spirits go to the Lord. The separation continues until the resurrection (John 5:28–29).

Our resurrection body is our earthly body, glorified. The

body we receive in the resurrection will have the same qualities as the glorified resurrection body of Christ (1 John 3:2).

Christ's resurrection body was not a wholly different body but rather, the same body He had before His crucifixion. It was in a glorified state, however. The wounds of His crucifixion were still visible. He could be touched and handled; He looked human in every regard. Jesus conversed a long time with the disciples on the road to Emmaus and they never once questioned His humanity (Luke 24:13–18). He ate real, earthly food with His disciples on another occasion (Luke 24:41–43). Even so, His body had unique otherworldly properties that allowed Him to pass through solid walls (John 20:19), appear seemingly out of nowhere (Luke 24:36), and ascend directly into heaven in bodily form (Luke 24:51; Acts 1:9). Our bodies will be like His. They will be real, physical, genuinely human bodies, yet wholly perfected and glorified. Paul wrote of this: "As we have borne the image of the man of dust, we shall also bear the image of the heavenly Man [Jesus Christ]" (1 Cor. 15:49).

The apostle Paul likened the death of our physical bodies to a seed planted in the earth. He wrote to the Corinthians: "Someone will say, 'How are the dead raised up? And with what body do they come?' Foolish one, what you sow is not made alive unless it dies. And what you sow, you do not sow that body that shall be, but mere grain—perhaps wheat or some other grain. But God gives it a body as He pleases, and to each seed its own body" (1 Cor. 15:35–38).

Every seed contains the pattern for the plant that grows from it. For example, all the genetic code for an entire oak tree is contained inside an acorn. Likewise, our resurrection bodies will bear a resemblance to the body that is buried, but with far greater glory. The resurrection body has none of the flaws of the old, but rather, is a perfect representation of what God created our body to be like apart from the influence of sin, disease, and all the frailties, flaws, and weaknesses of this earthly existence. Paul wrote, "The body is sown in corruption, it is raised in incorruption. It is sown in dishonor, it is raised in glory. It is sown in weakness, it is raised in power. It is sown a natural body, it is raised a spiritual body" (1 Cor. 15:42–44).

No wrinkles. No receding hairlines. No sickness. No evidence of injury, disease, or allergies. None of these things belong to a glorified resurrection body! The resurrection body can eat—but won't need to. It will be able to move at will through space and matter. It will be ageless and not know pain, tears, sorrow, sickness, decay, decline of any kind, or death. The only physical feature carried from earth to heaven will be the scars of Jesus—as eternal memorials to His sin-bearing sacrifice for us.

Scripture compares the glorified body to the shining of the moon and stars: "Those who are wise shall shine like the brightness of the firmament, and those who turn many to righteousness like the stars forever and ever" (Dan. 12:3).

The fullness of your identity. The New Testament indicates that our identities remain unchanged in heaven. While preparing for the Passover, Jesus took a cup and said to His disciples, "Take this [cup] and divide it among yourselves; for I say to you, I will not drink of the fruit of the vine until the kingdom of God comes" (Luke 22:17–18). Jesus was promising that He and his disciples would drink the fruit of the vine together again—in heaven. Elsewhere, Jesus made a similar but even more definite promise: "Many will come from east and west, and sit down with Abraham, Isaac, and Jacob in the kingdom of heaven" (Matt. 8:11). Jesus clearly expects us to *recognize* Abraham and Isaac and Jacob. All the redeemed will maintain their identities forever, but in fullness and perfection. In heaven, we will be able to have fellowship with any of the saints we choose.

Moses and Elijah appeared with Christ on the Mount of Transfiguration. Even though they had died centuries before, they maintained a clear identity—and Peter, James, and John evidently recognized them for who they were (Matt. 17:3–4). We will be able to recognize people we've never seen before in heaven. There will be something about their identity that will be lasting, distinctive, and recognizable to us.

When the Sadducees tried to trap Jesus about the resurrection, Jesus cited God's words to Moses in Exodus 3:6: "I am the God of your father—the God of Abraham, the God of Isaac, and the God of Jacob." Jesus noted, "God is not the God of the dead, but of the living" (Matt. 22:32). Jesus was clearly stating that Abraham, Isaac, and Jacob were still *living*, and God continued to be their God. They had identifiable, distinct identities.

You will know your child. Your child will know you. Even if

your child never saw your face or you never saw the face of your child, your child will know you and you will know your child.

The apostle Paul wrote of the Lord's appearing and the resurrection of the saints who have died by saying, "We who are alive and remain shall be caught up together with them in the clouds to meet the Lord in the air. And thus we shall always be with the Lord. Therefore comfort one another with these words" (1 Thess. 4:17–18). Comfort comes with the anticipation of reunion with our loved ones. We will be joined together and then live together forever in a depth of fellowship and understanding we have never known on this earth.

Theologian A. A. Hodge once wrote about our lives in heaven:

Heaven, as the eternal home of the divine Man and of all the redeemed members of the human race, must necessarily be thoroughly human in its structure, conditions, and activities. Its joys and its occupations must all be rational, moral, emotional, voluntary, and active. There must be the exercise of all faculties, the gratification of all tastes, the development of all talent capacities, the realization of all ideals. The reason, the intellectual curiosity, the imagination, the aesthetic instincts, the holy affections, the social affinities, the inexhaustible resources of strength and power native to the human soul, must all find in heaven exercise and satisfaction.[1]

Everything that is good about being a human being will be *gloriously good* in heaven!

Unbroken Fellowship with Our Heavenly Father

Without question, the most marvelous aspect of heaven will be unbroken fellowship with God our heavenly Father! This is heaven's supreme delight.

Our fellowship with God the Father will be perfect, unhindered, and unclouded by any sin or darkness.

On the night before His crucifixion, Jesus prayed for His disciples, including you and me, "that *they all may be one, as You, Father, are in Me, and I in You; that they also may be one in Us*, that the world may believe that You sent Me. And the glory which You gave Me I have given them, that they may be one just as We are one: *I in them, and You in Me; that they may be made perfect in one*, and that the world may know that You have sent Me, and have loved them as You have loved Me. Father, I desire that they also whom You gave Me may be with Me where I am, that they may behold My glory which You have given Me; for You loved Me before the foundation of the world" (John 17:21–24, emphasis added). Jesus desired that we have perfect fellowship with Him and the Father and that we experience the same kind of unity with the Father that He experienced!

This is such an incredibly profound concept that there's no way our finite minds can begin to appreciate it. We will be like Christ. We will be *with* Christ. We will enjoy unbroken and unfettered fellowship with God the Father. What glory that will be!

In heaven, we will see the Lord face-to-face. We will be able to see God's glory unveiled in its fullness. That will be a more pleasing, spectacular sight than anything we have known or could ever imagine on earth. No earthly pleasure can even begin to compare to the privilege and ecstasy of an unhindered view of His divine glory. Jesus said very clearly, "Blessed are the pure in heart, for they shall see God" (Matt. 5:8).

This close fellowship with the Lord has always been the deepest longing of the redeemed soul. The psalmist said, "As the deer pants for the water brooks, so pants my soul for You, O God. My soul thirsts for God, for the living God" (Ps. 42:1–2). Philip, speaking for all the disciples, said to Jesus, "Show us the Father, and it is sufficient for us" (John 14:8). Revelation 22:3–5 promises us the fulfillment of this great desire of the redeemed heart: "The throne of God and of the Lamb shall be in it, and His servants shall serve Him. They shall see His face, and His name shall be on their foreheads. There shall be no night there: They need no lamp nor light of the sun, for the Lord God gives them light. And they shall reign forever and ever."

As those redeemed by the Lord, our highest satisfaction will be standing before God the Father and His Son, Jesus Christ, in perfect uprightness. We will have an undiminished, unwearied sight of His infinite glory and beauty, and that alone will bring us infinite and eternal delight.

What a glorious existence your child has in heaven! What a glorious reunion and fellowship you will have together for all eternity!

SEVEN

Why Did My Child Have to Die?

TO TEST THE GENUINENESS OF A DIAMOND, JEWELERS often place it in clear water, which causes a real diamond to sparkle with special brilliance. An imitation stone, in contrast, has almost no sparkle. When an imitation stone and a real diamond are placed side by side in clear water, even an untrained eye can easily tell the difference.

It is in the throes of real-life tragedy that genuine Christians are easily distinguished from those who merely profess faith in Christ. There is a noticeable difference in radiance. How a person handles trouble reveals whether a person's faith is living or dead, genuine or imitation, saving or nonsaving.

This seems especially true when a child dies. Those parents who have the hope of heaven in their hearts, and who firmly believe their child is safe in the arms of God, are parents who grieve and long for their child—and yet, at the same time, they have a radiance about their faith that God is sovereign, God has a plan for their eternal reunion with their child, God has a purpose in all He does, and God will one day turn even this heartache into joy.

For some couples, the tragedy of losing a baby is compounded by the death of *another* child some time later. That was the case for Andrea and Steve. Steve works with me in the "Grace to You" radio ministry, so he and his family are especially precious to me.

After their first child, Andrew, died as a baby, Andrea was diagnosed with myotonic dystrophy—a genetic disease that is often passed on to children. Andrea's myotonic dystrophy probably started manifesting itself in her teen or early adult years, but her condition was not severe. At times Steve noted that Andrea didn't seem to be working as hard as her mother, two sisters, his own mom, or his own two sisters—all of whom were very industrious. He chalked up her failure to get a chore done as laziness, unaware that there were physiological factors that impacted her strength and energy level.

Steve was grateful for the diagnosis that came in the aftermath of Andrew's death because it gave him a new understanding and empathy for Andrea. He believed that it was an act of God's mercy to reveal Andrea's disease, and he felt that the Bible commanded him to live with Andrea in an understanding way, period. He became a much more understanding husband, which his wife greatly appreciated!

Steve has written, "My becoming more understanding is a direct consequence of having a child born with a disease that ultimately took his life. That's definitely a good result from our son's short life that God allowed us to see."

Another blessing that came to Steve and Andrea after Andrew's death was that the two of them experienced an even stronger marriage. They had always been close, but Andrew's life and death brought them even closer. That is not something that happens by accident. In fact, the statistics as a whole would predict the opposite. Many couples are torn apart by the death of a child, and especially so if one of the parents seems to be at fault—even if that "fault" is owing to a genetic disease that had been undiagnosed.

After the diagnosis of myotonic dystrophy, Steve and Andrea became pregnant again and their baby girl, Karlie, was born. She lived for twenty-two hours.

Steve wrote this about his baby daughter:

In a way, she was even more *my* baby than Andrea's. Andrea was able to spend much more time with Andrew during the two months he lived in the hospital—more time than I— and in some ways, I believe the loss of Andrew was more profound for her. In Karlie's case, I was the primary parent "on duty" for the whole of Karlie's life.

For much of the twenty-two hours Karlie lived, Andrea was heavily medicated from her C-section surgery. I was the only parent fully aware of what Karlie was going through. Even as we spent time with Karlie's body shortly after she died, Andrea was more asleep than awake. I found myself sitting there in a hospital room—my wife basically unconscious—with a cute but lifeless little person in my arms. I knew with great certainty that Andrea would not give birth to any more children. We had no children at home—no little ones to hold on to or take comfort in. During those minutes, as I sat in great sadness holding the lifeless body of my daughter, I had an overwhelming sense that God was holding *me*.

I'm not saying that I had some profound revelation in that hour. I simply had a great sense of peace that was beyond anything I can fully describe. I didn't fall apart emotionally. I knew I had no reason to do so. I had a hope deep within. I also knew that these responses of peace and hope weren't my natural mindset, but rather, the work of the Holy Spirit.

The hospital staff allowed us to spend an hour or two with Karlie's body. During that time, a pastor from our church called. We had been in touch with him—he knew Karlie had been born and was in serious condition, but at the time he called, he didn't know she had died. He listened to me explain how Karlie had begun failing a few hours before she died. I told him that I had been allowed to stay literally five feet from her bed even as the doctor, the respiratory therapist, and several nurses intensely worked to save her. I also told him that as Karlie was slipping away, I had a deep knowing in my spirit that God was in control of all things, including all that was unfolding before my eyes. I don't think I actually prayed in those minutes—I don't know that there was anything that I could have articulated to the Lord. I simply tried to take in all I could about my daughter's final minutes on this earth and deep within me, I knew that God is sovereign, and in the face of that abiding truth, I had great calm.

Two things have been very important to Steve and Andrea in the aftermath of the death of both their precious babies.

Steve says, "God had His people in the neonatal intensive care unit (NICU) to encourage and comfort us. One of those people, a respiratory therapist, has become an especially good friend. I do not at all think it was an accident that he was the respiratory therapist on duty the night Andrew was born, the night Andrew died about two months later, the night our daughter Karlie was born, or the night our daughter died. Andrea and I see him as a providential treasure. He provided unique comfort to us because he was such a like-minded brother in Christ.

"God also sent comfort to us in the form of fellow believers at our church. One couple, who had lost a child just the year before, offered us great comfort and encouragement."

Something that was vital to Steve and Andrea was an opportunity to present the gospel to unbelievers in the aftermath of their children's deaths. Steve told me, "We're thankful God has graciously shown us some of the good things that can come from a baby's death. A number of unbelievers came to the services for our children and at the services, they heard the gospel. The deaths of our children have given us several opportunities to answer the common question 'How did you get through that?' We can answer boldly, giving witness to God's love and grace, because they ask!"

Steve and Andrea are exploring the possibility of adopting a child. They know that their two children—Andrew and Karlie—are safe in the arms of God, eternally secure in their glorious heavenly home. Their hope is that they will be allowed to raise the children of others—very likely the children of parents who do not know the Lord's salvation—so that these little ones might grow in the nurture and admonition of the Lord. What a tremendous ministry adopting can be!

Why have I shared Steve and Andrea's story with you? In part because their experience touches on so many of the answers to the question "Why did my child have to die?"

Let me cover some of those answers a little more directly.

We Live in a Fallen World

Every person who lives in this world endures some measure of trouble. That is the consequence of the Fall, the natural result of sinful human nature and a world and society corrupted by iniquity. The prophet Isaiah declared, "They will look to the earth, and see trouble and darkness, gloom of anguish" (Isa. 8:22).

Even those who deeply love God and have been faithful in serving Him all their lives are not exempt from trouble. Difficult times are inevitable (1 Cor. 7:28). Jesus confirmed to His disciples, "In the world you will have tribulation" (John 16:33). Jesus wept when He saw Mary and the friends of her brother Lazarus grieving over Lazarus's death (John 11:35). He grieved at Judas's betrayal (John 13:21). Jesus' soul was "exceedingly sorrowful, even to death" as He prayed in the Garden of Gethsemane, anticipating the horror of being separated from the Father as He took on the sin of the world (Matt. 26:38). The apostle Paul wrote, "We are hard pressed on every side" (2 Cor. 4:8).

We simply cannot escape criticism, frustration, disappointment, physical pain, emotional pain, disease, injury, and eventually death. As Christians, we can also expect trouble solely *because* of our faith (John 15:20; 2 Tim. 3:12).

When parents experience the death of a child, one of the first questions they are likely to ask is, "Why did my child have to die?" I can tell you from many years of pastoring that the question is quite normal and natural; I understand the reasons couples ask it. Generally the emphasis in asking that question is "Why did *my* child have to die?" But the truth is, there is no easy answer to that question, and what we can say with certainty isn't usually very comforting to grieving parents. The answer begins with the fact that life is marked by difficulty and sorrow. We live in a fallen world. We live in a world flawed by disease and sin. Various aspects of the chemical, material, geophysical, and biological world have fallen into disarray since the Fall. Trouble comes to us as part of our human condition.

"But the Lord could have prevented this," a parent may counter.

Yes. God is omnipotent. He is also omniscient. As a result, some of His purposes and plans we cannot know this side of eternity. God may have allowed a child to die for reasons that will never be understood—reasons that may involve the lives of the parents, the lives of siblings, the life of the child himself, the lives of others unknown by the parents or child.

There is a question even more potent than the question "Why did my child have to die?" That question is "What does God desire for me to do in the midst of this tragedy?" The question of "Why?" has no satisfactory answer. The question of "What now?" can turn a person from grief to action, from loss to healing, from sorrow to joy, and from feelings of utter devastation to feelings of purpose. "Why?" is a question that keeps a person looking backward in time. "What now?" is a question that moves a person toward the future.

Eight Purposes for Trials and Tragedies

Scripture points to at least eight purposes behind the Lord's allowing trials and tragedies to come our way. They can help you draw meaning and purpose from your difficult experience.

1. To test the strength of our faith. Sorrowful experiences give us a means of taking spiritual inventory of our own lives. Do we wallow in resentment, bitterness, or self-pity when trouble comes? Or do we turn more and more to the Lord and rely on Him with increasing dependence and humility? The answer tells us something about where we are in our faith, and where we need to grow.

In His omniscience, God knows our hearts. What He desires is that we also know our own hearts! In knowing our own hearts, we then bear responsibility for repenting in areas where we need to repent, in trusting God for His grace in ways we may not have trusted God previously, and in turning to God with a humble, dependent spirit instead of pride and independence.

2. To remind us not to let our trust in the Lord turn into presumption or spiritual self-satisfaction. The greater our blessings, the greater the tendency to look upon them as something we have earned or accomplished, rather than as a manifestation of God's grace. Paul said he felt the primary reason he had been given a "thorn in the flesh" was so he might not become "exalted above measure" in his own mind and heart (2 Cor. 12:7).

3. To wean us from our dependence on worldly things. Difficult experiences tend to turn our hearts and our attention to those things that are truly eternal and matter most in life. Material resources so often prove themselves inadequate when tragedy strikes. At times, there is no amount of medicine, money, or *anything* man-made that can make a difference between life and death. We are brought to the point of recognizing that only spiritual values are lasting. All things that are truly important have their beginning and ending in Christ Jesus.

4. To call us to heavenly hope. The harder a trial becomes and the longer it lasts, the more we look forward to being with the Lord and to the full redemption of our own bodies and of the entire creation. We hope for the fulfillment of all that He has planned and prepared. Paul wrote to the church at Rome:

> For I consider that the sufferings of this present time are not worthy to be compared with the glory which shall be revealed in us. For the earnest expectation of the creation eagerly waits for the revealing of the sons of God. For the creation was subjected to futility, not willingly, but because of Him who subjected it in hope; because the creation itself also will be delivered from the bondage of corruption into the glorious liberty of the children of God. For we know that the whole creation groans and labors with birth pangs together until now. Not only that, but we also who have the firstfruits of the Spirit, even we ourselves groan within ourselves, eagerly waiting for the adoption, the redemption of our body. For we were saved in this hope, but hope that is seen is not hope; for why does one still hope for what he sees? But if we hope for what we do not see, we eagerly wait for it with perseverance. (Rom. 8:18–25)

Note again the last line of the passage above. When we have hope, we are more likely to persevere in doing and believing those things we know are pleasing to the Lord. We wait with both eagerness and perseverance. Paul also wrote these encouraging words:

> We also believe and therefore speak, knowing that He who raised up the Lord Jesus will also raise us up with Jesus, and will present us with you. For all things are for your sakes, that grace, having spread through the many, may cause thanksgiving to abound to the glory of God.
>
> Therefore we do not lose heart. Even though our outward man is perishing, yet the inward man is being renewed day by day. For our light affliction, which is but for a moment, is working for us a far more exceeding and eternal weight of glory. (2 Cor. 4:13–17)

Time and again, parents who have lost a child have told me that they have a new eagerness to be with the Lord in heaven so they might be reunited with their child. They have a greater ability to endure the hardships of this life because they have an insight into eternity. They persevere with greater enduring power because they have a new hope for the glory that lies ahead.

5. To reveal what we really love. Abraham deeply loved his son. The Lord recognized that love in calling to Abraham and commanding him, "Take now your son, your only son Isaac, whom you love, and go to the land of Moriah, and offer him there" (Gen. 22:2). Abraham's willingness to obey God was not only evidence of his faith in God, but also of his supreme love for the Lord. Jesus, in speaking to His disciples on the night before the Crucifixion, said repeatedly to them, "If anyone loves Me, he will keep My word" (John 14:23; see also John 14:15, 21).

Do we love God more than any human being? Do we love God's glorious purpose in heaven for our child more than our earthly plans? That is how God calls us to love Him. Do we love God to the point that we are willing to obey Him in *all* things? That is what God calls us to do. Tragedies often show us whether we have that kind of love for God.

6. To teach us to value God's blessings. Our senses tell us to value those things that give us pleasure and ease. Our ability to reason tells us to value those things that bring treasure, position, and power. It is through trials that our faith tells us to value the spiritual things of God—His Word, His care, His provision, His strength, and, most of all, His salvation.

The psalmist—who had known times of hardship and times of great blessing—wrote:

> Because Your lovingkindness is better than life,
> My lips shall praise You.
> Thus I will bless You while I live;
> I will lift up my hands in Your name.
> My soul shall be satisfied as with marrow and fatness,
> And my mouth shall praise You with joyful lips.
> (Ps. 63:3–5)

Nothing is more valuable than God's loving-kindness—His presence with us, and His forgiveness extended so mercifully and freely toward us.

When we lose a child, our focus is turned away from the pleasures and agendas of this world and toward a heavenly joy and the heavenly agenda. Our priorities fall into line. Our values are readjusted to place proper emphasis on those things that are of God.

Our response to God's blessings must be ongoing praise and thanksgiving. The thankful heart is the "remembering heart"; the heart of praise remembers all that the Lord has done, is doing, and has promised to do.

7. To enable us to better endure future trials and difficulties.
Not long ago I heard about a woman who was diagnosed with cancer two years after she lost a child. Then, while she was still in treatment for the cancer, her mother and father were both killed in an automobile accident. It seemed that trouble was being heaped upon trouble in her life.

She told a pastor who visited her in the hospital where she was undergoing a round of chemotherapy treatment, "I don't fear death in the way I once did. I don't fear pain and physical difficulty the way I once did. I experienced far more than watching a child die with an illness. As I watched my child get thinner and thinner and seem to waste away into death, I saw the Lord grow stronger and stronger in my life. He became more powerful and awesome week by week as my Savior, Redeemer,

Healer, and Lord. The darker the days became as my child grew sicker and sicker, the brighter the Lord shone in my life. He continues to shine now."

She continued, "I intend to recover from this disease called cancer so I can continue to be a mother to my other two children. I intend to live my life victoriously in Christ Jesus until the day He calls me home. But if He should call me home sooner rather than later, I'm ready for that as well. He has shown me His sustaining grace and love, and He continues to reveal His grace and love to me every day. I know Him in ways I didn't know Him a few years ago. I have full confidence that He will never leave me nor forsake me. He will only hold me tighter and tighter in His everlasting embrace."

What a beautiful and powerful testimony that woman has! As it turns out, she is alive fifteen years after her cancer treatment. Her older son is in graduate school. Her older daughter has married and has a baby. And guess who is baby-sitting that little girl while her mother goes back to college to finish her degree? A very loving and faith-filled grandmother! This woman has been forged into a pillar of strength by the Lord's abiding presence through trial after trial. Which leads me to an eighth way trials and tragedies produce something good in our lives.

8. To help us develop "enduring strength" so we might be of even greater use in God's kingdom. The writer of Hebrews speaks of the godly men and women "who through faith subdued kingdoms, worked righteousness, obtained promises, stopped the mouths of lions, quenched the violence of fire, escaped the edge of the sword, out of weakness were made strong" (Heb. 11:33–34).

In nearly every case of which I am personally aware, parents who have lost a child have developed a stronger, more effective ministry in helping other parents who are going through difficult times with a sick child or who have more recently lost a child. God equips His saints, in part, through experience. It is as we trust God in our own trials and tragedies that we are better prepared to help others trust God.

The woman I told you about above not only helps her family and cares for her grandchild on a daily basis, but she heads the hospital-visitation program in her church. She personally visits the children who are ill and in the hospital because, as she says, "I have something to say to their parents. The parents know my faith is real. They know my hope is genuine. They not only know it from the Scriptures I share and the prayers I pray, but they know it from my experience. I can tell them with great confidence that God does not fail, He does not disappoint, and He does not abandon us in our sorrow."

The apostle Paul wrote to the Corinthians:

Blessed be the God and Father of our Lord Jesus Christ, the Father of mercies and God of all comfort, who comforts us in all our tribulation, that we may be able to comfort those who are in any trouble, with the comfort with which we ourselves are comforted by God. For as the sufferings of Christ abound in us, so our consolation also abounds through Christ. (2 Cor. 1:3–5)

I do not know the precise reasons God allowed your baby to die, but I do know that if you will allow Him to do His work in you and through you, you will learn some eternally valuable lessons and grow in ways that are spiritually and eternally beneficial. I encourage you today:

Examine your own heart. Ask the Lord how He desires for you to grow in your faith. If there are areas in which you need to repent, do so. If there are areas of personal spiritual discipline in which you know you need to grow, place a greater emphasis on those disciplines in your life. Make it your prayer: "Lord, I believe. Help my unbelief."

Put your full trust in the Lord. Ask the Lord to reveal to you the ways you may have been trusting your own talents or skills, reasoning power, intellectual ability, or personality—instead of trusting God. Make it your prayer: "Lord, help me to trust You in *all* things at *all* times, regardless of outer circumstances or consequences."

Check your priorities in life. Are you placing highest value on those things that truly matter the most? Make it your prayer: "Lord, help me to see my life as You see it and to put things into the priority order You desire."

Choose hope. Ask the Lord to turn your discouragement into encouragement by giving you opportunities to express hope to others. As you voice your hope in heaven and your hope of God's glory being revealed in all creation one day, you will find yourself encouraged. Make it your prayer: "Lord, let me catch a glimpse of all You have prepared for my child and for me in eternity."

Evaluate what you love most. Are you loving people or things? Are you loving self or others? Are you loving the Lord for who He is, or because of what you hope He'll do for you? Give yourself a "heart checkup." Make it your prayer: "Lord, I love You. Help me to love You with a purer, deeper, and more all-encompassing love. Help me to keep my eyes on You."

Place a new emphasis on praise and thanksgiving in your life. A thankful heart is a heart that values what God does, what God provides, what God gives and, most of all, who God is. It is a heart that both recognizes and cherishes the *spiritual* blessings that only God can give. Make it your prayer, "Lord, let me love what You love. Let me receive all that You desire to give me. Let me be satisfied with all that You are."

Ask the Lord to make you stronger and more able to persevere. Ask the Lord to give you courage for what lies ahead. Make it your prayer: "Help me, Lord, to prepare for what You have already prepared for me."

Look for opportunities to minister to others. Ask the Lord to reveal to you the ways in which you can help others in need, and to direct you to those who need your words of faith, love, and encouragement. Make it your prayer: "Lord, make me a blessing to others today."

How Are We to Respond?

Every parent who loses a child needs to take time to grieve the loss of that child. There comes a time, however, when grieving needs to end. Scripture tells us that there are at least five keys to our being made whole after the death of a little one.

Joy. First, we must *choose* to have a joyful attitude. Joy is not something we automatically feel or don't feel. Many times joy is a choice we must make. It is a decision that comes from the will. We can choose the attitude we will have. We can choose whether we will laugh or frown. We can choose whether we will praise or keep silent. We can choose whether we will express joy to others or express sorrow. James wrote: "Count it all joy when you fall into various trials" (James 1:2).

"But I don't *feel* joyful!" you may say. "Isn't it hypocritical to express something you don't feel?"

No. We are challenged by Scripture to *choose* how we will feel. James didn't say, "*Feel* it all joy"; he said, "*Count* it all joy." We are to voice praise and thanksgiving to the Lord and to express our hope and joy *first*. The feelings follow. The world waits for feelings and then acts. The Christian is called to act first, knowing that feelings will come as a consequence of action.

Patience. Second, we must *choose* to believe that God has a timetable and purpose for all things. We must choose to be patient as we await the revealing and the fulfilling of God's purposes. James wrote, "The testing of your faith produces patience. But let patience have its perfect work, that you may be perfect and complete, lacking nothing" (James 1:3–4).

There's an old saying that time heals all wounds. Some old sayings simply aren't true. Time may cause a hurtful memory to fade a little, but *time* doesn't heal. *God* heals. He heals us, in part, as we trust Him to *be* God in all things, at all times, and for all His sovereign purposes, some of which may not be revealed to us in this lifetime. We must *choose* to be patient in trusting God to act according to His timetable and according to His chosen methods.

This life—and everything we know as "time"—is not something we can even calculate in relationship to eternity. Our life is but "a vapor that appears for a little time and then vanishes away" (James 4:14). God deals in the timetable of eternity. His purposes are eternal. We must choose to see things from His perspective as best we can, and trust Him for what we do not see and cannot know.

Wisdom. Third, we must seek wisdom. There are some things we may need to know about why a child has died—in order to learn lessons of eternal consequence. There are some things we are wise to let go as we trust God.

Some situations may not have answers. Some solutions may

not yet be available. Some problems may remain mysteries. Ask the Lord to reveal to you what it is that He desires for you to know, especially ways in which He desires for you to grow spiritually as a result of your experience.

And most important, ask God for wisdom with a full expectancy of your faith that He will give you wisdom. James tells us,

> If any of you lacks wisdom, let him ask of God, who gives to all liberally and without reproach, and it will be given to him. But let him ask in faith, with no doubting, for he who doubts is like a wave of the sea driven and tossed by the wind. For let not that man suppose that he will receive anything from the Lord; he is a double-minded man, unstable in all his ways. (James 1:5–8)

A submissive will. God's desire for us always is to submit our wills to His will. Perhaps nothing is more difficult. Our tendency as human beings is to want to be number one. Pride is extremely difficult to lay down.

Scripture tells us, however, that God cannot do His perfect and complete work in us and through us unless we are willing to submit ourselves to His will.

In James 1:3–4 quoted above, to be "perfect" means to be fully developed. God calls us to *maturity*. That speaks of completion—of being whole or entire—lacking nothing. That is God's plan for each of us.

I have met a number of women who simply do not believe they can be "whole" unless they give birth to a child. Their identity—their sense of value and meaning—is wrapped up in being able to bear a child. When they do not conceive, do not carry a child to delivery, or have a child who is stillborn or dies shortly after birth, they are devastated beyond measure. Many remain inconsolable and increasingly desperate to bear a child.

Such a woman needs to ask herself very candidly, "Am I relying on the birth of a child to make me whole or to feel complete? Do I believe that giving birth and becoming a mother will make me more mature in the eyes of others and, therefore, worthy of more respect? Do I believe that by giving birth, I will gain the admiration of others?" God's desire for each of us, not just expectant mothers, is that we will understand that He and He alone is the author and finisher of our lives. He is the One who gives us our identity, our value, and our sense of belonging. He alone is the One who makes us whole and raises us up to maturity in the image of Christ Jesus.

In some cases, God's will does not seem to be that a woman, or a couple, should bear children physically—but rather, His will seems to be that they adopt babies who are in desperate need of a loving, Christian home. In other cases, God's will is that a couple devote themselves to the *spiritual* birthing of souls. Their purpose is winning souls or discipling believers rather than child-rearing.

Ask the Lord what He wants for you, and then submit to His will. Do all that you can do—and then trust God to do what

He knows is best for your ultimate fulfillment, joy, and purpose. He has created you with a purpose. Ask Him to reveal that purpose to you so you might pursue it with your whole heart, mind, and soul.

A believing heart. Above all, the Lord asks us to have a believing heart in all situations and in spite of all consequences. He calls us to trust Him to be generous toward us and to give us all things that are for our benefit because He "gives to all liberally and without reproach" (James 1:5–8).

The Lord knows what you need, and He desires for you to receive it. In many cases, however, He also requires that you *ask* Him for what you desire—not so He will know your desire but so *you* will know what it is you are desiring. Many times we don't truly know our own hearts until we give voice to our own feelings, needs, and longings.

Jesus said:

Ask, and it will be given to you; seek, and you will find; knock, and it will be opened to you. For everyone who asks receives, and he who seeks finds, and to him who knocks it will be opened. Or what man is there among you who, if his son asks for bread, will give him a stone? Or if he asks for a fish, will he give him a serpent? If you then, being evil, know how to give good gifts to your children, how much more will your Father who is in heaven give good things to those who ask Him!" (Matt. 7:7–11)

Ask the Lord for what you desire. And then, be willing to believe God that the answer He gives is the answer that is truly best for you. God may not answer "Yes"—but you can trust that if His answer is "No" or "Not now" or "When certain conditions are met," that answer is the *best* answer.

Pursue God's best, and trust God to give you His best.

Becoming Whole

As you choose to live your life with joy, as you choose to patiently await the fulfillment of God's timing in your life, as you choose to seek wisdom, as you continue to submit to the Lord and to trust God in all things—you *will* be made whole. Your broken heart will be mended. Your life will be put back together. You will be able to let go of the "why" questions. You will be able to face the future with courage, strength, and stronger faith. You will have a renewed sense of purpose and a greater faith to share with others.

I encourage you to pray today:

Lord, help me to express the joy that is befitting a Christian. Help me to trust You with the timetable of my life and the lives of all those I love. Help me to have a more eternal perspective on what happens to me and to those I love. Help me to learn and to discover what it is that You want me to know. Give me Your wisdom. Help me to submit myself to Your will and to do so completely, in every area of my life. Help me to trust You that You know what is best for me, You desire to bring about what is best for my life, and You are at work causing all things to come together for my eternal good and the eternal good of all those I love. I pray this with faith, Lord. I look for the answers You will give as I pray in Jesus' name. Amen.

EIGHT

How Shall We Minister to Those Who Are Grieving?

A NUMBER OF PARENTS WHO HAVE LOST INFANTS HAVE shared with me through the years that they received wonderful, wise, and godly counsel after their babies died. Others, however, have told me they received very bad or weak counsel. In some cases, what people said or did only added to their pain and confusion. In this chapter, I want to portray to you the type of ministry I hope you will seek out in your loss. Knowing that the Lord very likely will call upon you to minister to others in the future, I also want to help you in a very practical way to become a wonderful, wise, and godly counselor to others. Let me begin by sharing with you the story of a woman named Lisa.

Lisa awoke with cramps. Her first thought was, *Heartburn!* She knew she was pregnant—only about three months along— but she didn't connect the cramping with her pregnancy. She hadn't experienced any such twinges in her abdomen with her first pregnancy, and she quickly concluded her trouble was intestinal. *That Italian food we had last night was pretty spicy,* she thought and went back to sleep. She took a couple of pills that her physician had prescribed as being "pregnancy safe" in case she had indigestion, which she seemed to have fairly frequently since the birth of her son two years earlier. She was grateful that her son had spent the night at his grandmother's house—a gift from her mother so she and her husband might actually have a "date night."

Three hours later, Lisa again awoke, this time to intense cramps. She knew something was seriously wrong. Overwhelmingly weak, she barely made it to the phone to call her husband at work. He raced home, scooped her up and placed her in the backseat of the car, and drove her immediately to the hospital. Within an hour, she and her husband heard four words they had never imagined they would hear in their lives: "You've lost your baby."

It took several hours of counseling by a nurse at the hospital for Lisa to come to some peace about the fact that even if she had experienced the cramps at the hospital, nothing could have been done to keep the baby from miscarrying.

Two days later, Lisa saw her physician and came away comforted by his telling her that in all likelihood she would be able to conceive again and bear a child—but to wait a while. She was anything but comforted, however, by what a nurse in the physician's office said to her. This particular nurse was not a part of the regular staff—she had come in for a couple of days because the regular nurses were either away on vacations that could not be rescheduled or were sick. The substitute nurse said, "Dearie, count your blessings. What you lost wasn't really a baby; it was only a mass of tissue. And apparently something wasn't right with it. You could have developed a very deformed baby if you hadn't lost that tissue."

Lisa was deeply troubled by the nurse's remarks. Was it some misplaced maternal instinct that caused her to feel such a sense of loss? Was her profound sense of grief uncalled for? Far from being comforted by the nurse's words, she recoiled from the notion that she and Greg had lost nothing more than a "mass of tissue." The thought of dismissing their loss so lightly only increased the pain in her heart.

Later she discussed her feelings with Greg. Although he had tried to be strong and stoic in order to be a support to Lisa through their ordeal, he wept with her when she repeated what the nurse had said. It struck him as calloused and heartless that anyone would try to assuage their grief by denying that an unborn child was even a true person.

Together, Lisa and Greg sought their pastor's counsel. He reminded them of several important principles:

1. The child who died was a *person with a soul*, regardless of the age of the child at the time of death. The child was created by God for a specific purpose known only to God. The child has an eternal destiny and lives today in the presence of God the Father.

2. We who are alive and remain on this earth have a responsibility to trust Christ, to live for Him, and to be faithful evangelists

to friends and loved ones. Meanwhile, we eagerly await the time when we will join this child in heaven.

3. God is sovereign and perfect in all that He does and is. We must recognize that in many situations, we cannot know His full purposes or plan. But we can trust that His purposes and plan are *perfect*. At times we need to remind ourselves of the Lord's words to us in Isaiah:

> "For My thoughts are not your thoughts,
> Nor are your ways My ways," says the LORD.
> "For as the heavens are higher than the earth,
> So are My ways higher than your ways,
> And My thoughts than your thoughts." (Isa. 55:8–9)

4. We need to remind ourselves that God not only is able to heal a broken heart, He delights in healing broken hearts and mending shattered lives. He can reinstill in us an enthusiasm for what remains ahead. He wants us to live in renewed joy and the hope of eternal life. He wants us to fully embrace the plans and purposes He has for us as we live out the remainder of our time on this earth.

5. And finally, we ought to be greatly comforted by the knowledge that this little one is in heaven, in the presence of Christ, enjoying all the wonders of that glorious place, free from all the troubles of this earth, dwelling in perfect bliss, surrounded by perfect love, and loving and worshiping Christ perfectly in return.

Certainly we need to give grieving parents a shoulder to cry on and time to grieve their loss. We need, at times, to be silently present with them, simply "there" for them, sharing in their sorrow (Rom. 12:15). We must not be glib or lighthearted in an attempt to elevate them from their sadness, but at the same time, we need to be encouraging and strong in our own faith. We need to point the grieving parent to God's love and mercy, His grace and sovereignty, and His challenges and commandments that direct us toward the future, not the past.

Acknowledge the Loss

Perhaps the greatest injustice we can do a grieving parent is to remain silent about the loss that has been experienced. Silence does little to heal. In many cases, refusing to address or acknowledge a loss can cause a parent to feel unwarranted guilt or shame.

"A pastor's wife just shouldn't lose a baby." That was the statement made by Flo after she miscarried her child after only two and a half months of pregnancy—in fact, the week after she learned she was pregnant. Flo's husband was a man who preached a strong message of faith being able to conquer all life's problems. Flo felt guilty, believing that in some way she had "let down" her husband and the truth of the gospel. For his part, her husband never mentioned to others the fact that she had been pregnant, had lost the baby while he was away preaching a revival at another church in another state, or that there was any reason for her to feel guilty or remorseful at this loss in her life.

Flo had told only her parents and one friend about her pregnancy. Rather than tell them she had miscarried, she followed up with them by saying, with as lighthearted a tone as she could, "It was a false alarm. No need to think about baby clothes!"

Flo fell silent about her pregnancy and her loss. She never mentioned the experience publicly. She never even acknowledged to her two older children that she had been pregnant. It was only years later when her grown daughter Beth lost her third child through miscarriage that Flo shared with her that she had been through the same experience. Mother and daughter grew even closer in the bond of tears and loss they shared. Flo also encouraged Beth to take a very different approach from the one she had taken.

"Talk to your husband and your friends about this," Flo advised. "Take time to mourn the loss of this little one."

Flo confessed to her daughter, "I never really mourned the loss of this baby. My miscarriage was an embarrassment to me. I felt that I had 'failed' God and your father in some way. It is only in the last year that I've come to realize the little baby I lost is still alive in heaven. That baby has a full-blown identity as a child of God, and I will see that little one again someday. In many ways, I have a great peace and joy—something I haven't had for more than thirty years—that a part of me is already in heaven."

Flo laughed a little when she shared with Beth, "I have

named that baby Terry—which could be the name for either a boy or a girl."

Why Terry? "Because," Flo explained, "I have to tarry a while longer on this earth before I get to be with this child."

Flo is not unlike many women, especially of her generation, who believe they have failed because they had a miscarriage. The greater truth of the Scripture is that *all* life is in the hands of God and that He is the author and finisher of every work He ordains. As I mentioned earlier, many parents today believe that they "create" their child. Nothing could be further from the truth. Certainly they were part of a process God used, but God alone creates life.

Flo experienced a great healing of her emotions when she was able to talk freely about the loss she had experienced. She and Beth were able to grieve together the loss of Beth's baby, which was Flo's grandbaby. In sharing their grief, they found they were also sharing their love. That is true in most situations—shared grief becomes a bond of shared love.

A Loss for the Entire Community

I want to share one more story with you because it covers so many of the wonderful things we can do as fellow Christians for those who have experienced the death of a child.

Dan and Pamela, two members of our church, wrote eloquently to me of the life and death of their infant son, Ryan. Each of them wrote about their experience, and I want to share both of their letters with you. Here is what Dan wrote from his perspective as a father:

"Awake or asleep we live together with Him." These are the words carved in bronze on my son's gravestone. They are the unshaken hope and comfort of Mom and Dad.

Ryan died in my arms six years ago. I held and kissed him until he stopped breathing. The medical staff at Children's Hospital made every heroic effort to save his life. Yet he was unable to survive the trauma of intestinal surgery. His heart simply gave out.

Ryan graced the earth for seven days. My wife's connection to him was longer and more profound. She carried him thirty-five weeks to delivery.

Without going into great detail, Ryan was born healthy. While small—under three pounds—his lungs were developed and he breathed without assistance. An intestinal infection on his sixth day changed that perspective. Our hearts were dashed over the next forty-eight hours as his condition seemingly stabilized then worsened repeatedly in what some might assess as a cruel rhythm. In the end, Ryan was spared a difficult life and ushered into God's presence.

God's will in suffering is often veiled in mystery. We rejoice that He allowed us to perceive the good that was wrought through Ryan's brief life. I came face-to-face with these unalterable truths:

First, I came face-to-face with the reality that God alone is sovereign. I am not. He controls every aspect of my future—from our family's health to our standard of living. I do not. As a man, it was easy to succumb to the "myth of control" and a sense of exaggerated importance. Any integrity, intellect, determination, creativity, or persuasion on my part, however, could not dictate an outcome here. I had no control. God did.

Second, Christ and His Word are sufficient. As the psalmist promised, "In God's presence is fullness of joy." His Word and its promises are reliable. While our faith was tested, our heavenly Father was found faithful. His grace proved sufficient. In our weakness His love and peace enveloped us. The mind of Christ kept any root of bitterness or self-pity from undermining our communion with God or each other. Any peace or strength we displayed were only a function of God's grace in our life. We were cradled by our great God of comfort.

Third, this trial enabled us to experience the unbridled love of the body of Christ. The perspective, presence, and love of Pastor MacArthur and Christian friends touched us deeply. We were loved in many tangible ways. To our great joy this did not go unnoticed by our unsaved friends and family members.

Fourth, the gospel was advanced because of Ryan's life. God's love and "His peace which surpasses all understanding" were real and on display. This gave us comfort as Ryan's death provided a platform to share God's truth and love. The gospel message was clearly presented at Ryan's memorial service and in many intimate conversations.

And finally, heaven is more real to us. Heaven is not a vague concept or mysterious destination anymore. We long for that day of communion with Christ and reunion with Ryan.

And here is what Pamela wrote of that same experience— what a tender message from the heart of a grieving mother:

When our daughter Megan Hannah was ten months old, we learned our second child was on the way. We were happy our little family was increasing in number. From the very beginning of the pregnancy, I remember telling Danny I felt an overwhelming sense the Lord was going to put our faith to the test. "I think we are going to go through the biggest trial of our lives." How and to what degree was unknown. The Lord was preparing us even in those early weeks.

I was four months along when our trial began to unfold. My first ultrasound showed something inconsistent, and my doctor referred me to an ultrasound specialist at Genetics Institute for a more in-depth ultrasound. I was terrified. We called family and friends asking for prayer. The appointment came and the ultrasound confirmed that a little more than half of my placenta had completely stopped functioning. The umbilical cord was not providing enough nourishment, blood, or oxygen for our baby to thrive. Our baby was grossly underdeveloped.

We endured genetics counseling with a specialist, which was horrifying. It was meant to be very helpful and informative. They counseled us on our "options" and blandly explained our baby was at high risk for what seemed like every imaginable long-term illness that would require extensive care: spina bifida, cystic fibrosis, and so forth. Chances were our baby was going to die before birth, at birth, or shortly after birth. The statistics were unbelievably high toward that end.

My doctor placed me on home bed rest and only allowed me to shower in the morning and use the rest room as needed. My only time out of the house was to go to a doctor's appointment. I had to rely on an intricate schedule of friends coming in shifts to take care of all the practical matters related to my child and my home.

Each visit to the specialist was an answer to prayer, however, and another chance to cling to God in prayer. Our little baby boy, as we found out, went from having a hole in his heart to having no hole in his heart, from having water around his brain to having no water around his brain, from having no growth rate at all to having grown, from having decreased flow of blood, oxygen, and nourishment to having increased flows, from having abnormally low fluid levels to having just the right amount. These are just a few of the examples of serious things that showed up each and every time we went to see the specialist. The specialist was always bewildered as to why these things cleared up. We knew why they cleared up, and we took opportunities to explain to him why! Our God was bigger than any of the life-threatening physical abnormalities we faced each time we went to see the specialist. We fervently brought every little detail before the

Lord, and by the time we would go to our next appointment, He had already done His work. We made sure it was a testimony to God and not anything we had done on our own. It wasn't "luck"—it was God being involved in every little detail of our son's knitting together.

We slowly started realizing the opportunities God was laying before us to share Christ with those we came into contact with and to be a good testimony of God's work in our lives. Our prayer lives were never stronger as we both prayed for our little son and for what the Lord would have for him and for us.

Home bed rest turned into hospital bed rest. I was hooked up to everything and monitored every fifteen minutes around the clock, being stuffed with up to five thousand calories a day. I received regular steroid shots to boost the development of our son's lungs as well. I was lonely for my family—I missed being a wife and mother.

After a little over three weeks in the hospital, the physicians determined that Ryan was at a higher risk being in the womb than delivered, so it was time for a C-section. This was it! All the prayers were said and it was time to see what the Lord had for us. My original due date was April 15 and our son, Ryan James, was born March 11, 1996. He was the tiniest little thing, weighing only two pounds and ten ounces, measuring fifteen inches. He did pretty well on his Apgar Tests and he was considered a "well preemie baby." He was in NICU doing well and I was recovering from surgery. We were emotionally, mentally, and spiritually relieved. The

Lord had seen us through all the ups and downs, and now we had little Ryan James and he would come home in a month. We were so incredibly thankful to our Jesus for bringing our little boy into this world. Ryan was tiny but healthy. He was our miracle baby. So many answered prayers, so much spiritual growth and reliance on the Lord—it was truly amazing! We felt blessed. Our trial finally seemed to be over.

I went home from the hospital while Ryan remained in the intensive care unit. On March 17, the NICU doctor in charge of little Ryan called and asked us to come down to the hospital. She said she needed to see us right away. What could possibly be wrong? She told us Ryan had NEC (necrotizing enterocolitis with perforation)—an intestinal bacterial infection. Our sweet little son was very sick. We were shellshocked. Our trial was supposed to be over, and here we were being told our son was in need of immediate emergency surgery so severe they couldn't even perform it there! He was stabilized several times until they were finally able to transport him to Children's Hospital. They explained they were going to have to remove most of his large intestine and part of his small intestine. The bacterial infection was gangrenous and spreading fast.

They performed the surgery on Ryan, but it was too much for his little two-pound, ten-ounce body to take, and he died of cardiac arrest with pulmonary hemorrhage. Ryan died in his daddy's arms on March 18, 1996. He was one week old.

I remember someone saying it was good that he passed on

before I could have become attached. I couldn't believe what I was hearing. Such thinking was ridiculous. My whole life for the past four months had revolved around Ryan. I knew his every little movement in my womb. His life began way before he ever came into this world. He had not been with me for just a week—he had been with me for months.

Throughout all these months, I felt as if our faith was being tested to the nth degree. At times, I didn't know where to turn. After Ryan died, I wondered if I was going crazy. What kept me from going over the edge?

God's Word proved itself to us again and again. His grace was, and is, sufficient. God was, and is, faithful to His promises. These three verses were of special comfort to us:

- My grace is sufficient for you, for My strength is made perfect in weakness. (2 Cor. 12:9)

- The LORD is near to those who have a broken heart. (Ps. 34:18)

- Now no chastening seems to be joyful for the present, but painful; nevertheless, afterward it yields the peaceable fruit of righteousness to those who have been trained by it. (Heb. 12:11)

At the time—and even now—my heart was broken, my sorrow deep. Even so, I knew deep within that Jesus *loved* us and He knew why He allowed this to happen. I kept reminding myself, "Not that I have already attained, or am already perfected; but I press on, that I may lay hold of that for which Christ Jesus has also laid hold of me" (Phil. 3:12). I believed God was doing His refining work in us. He was broadening our ability to minister to other families. He knew we could endure. I relied upon His Word: "We know that all things work together for good to those who love God, to those who are the called according to His purpose" (Rom. 8:28).

The most amazing revelation was that God's Word was real. The Bible wasn't just words anymore—they came alive! We owned them and we relied on them. We knew God's Word was "living and powerful" (Heb. 4:12). We had lived through it. God's grace *was* sufficient. He had sustained us. He had comforted us. He had provided for us. He had cared for us. He did love us. He was good to us. He knew exactly what we could handle, and He did not give us any more, or any less.

From an earthly perspective, losing a child is probably the worst thing that can happen to a family. Knowing the Lord through this, however, has brought blessing and purpose.

I can say this is a blessing for several reasons.

One, we know for certain, without a doubt, that Ryan is with Jesus and we will be reunited with him for eternity. Our life here is a dot on a time line that never ends. Our time here without him doesn't even compare to an eternity reunited with him. We still need to be on our knees for our three daughters He has entrusted to us. Megan has made a serious decision to follow Christ, has a clear understanding of sin, of God's forgiveness, and of what she needs to do now that she believes in Christ. We don't know for certain about our other two younger daughters. Their lives are ahead of them, and it is our deepest desire that they all grow up to know and love Jesus.

Two, this experience has been a blessing to us because we have a renewed hope and understanding about heaven. Heaven is that much sweeter because Ryan is there. My desire to be in heaven is much more intense. Heaven, in my mind, is right around the corner. I can't wait to be there.

And three, this was a blessing because so many friends ministered to us in so many tangible ways. Their help was a testimony of God's love, care, and concern for us. The body of Christ in action is truly amazing—we were blown away by their kindness. Friends took care of us in so many practical ways—from providing meals to baby-sitting—and also in spiritual ways by praying for us and standing with us—and they did this for an extended period of time. That is no small gift of love.

When we hear of someone losing their baby we know their pain, and it isn't easy because we are confronted with our own pain all over again. Yet, we have had opportunities to help other families through the death of a little one. Often, words are not spoken. Just the fact that they see us still functioning and loving each other is a witness to them that God has brought us through this experience and what He has done for us, He can and will do for them if they will only trust Him.

Ten months after Ryan passed away, I had a miscarriage. A

month later, we learned that we were expecting a baby—our precious Lauren Marie. I went through two more miscarriages before the Lord brought us Taryn Reece. Each pregnancy had its own trials, but through them all, I can say, "To Christ be the glory . . . amen!" Our reliance on the Lord and our relationship with Him have grown so much.

Dan and Pamela have seven children—three on this earth, their precious daughters. They know they have a son named Ryan James in heaven. But they also have three more children in heaven—the precious little ones they conceived who did not survive pregnancy. What a joyful reunion lies ahead for this family!

Let me point out several things to you from these letters written by this dear couple.

Presence. First, Christian friends were very "present" for Dan and Pamela. They were present in their lives in very practical ways—helping with baby-sitting, food, and home care.

God's Word. Second, the truth revealed in the Word of God was a vital source of strength for both parents. It is a source of strength to all who will turn to it in a time of need!

Be bold in sharing words of Scripture with those who are grieving. You don't need to preach a sermon. But you can say to a parent, "I found this verse of Scripture particularly encouraging, and I thought you might find it helpful"—and then share a verse of encouragement about God's abiding presence.

Hope of heaven. Third, the hope of heaven was and is very real to Dan and Pamela. What a wonderful thing when Christians can talk about heaven together! Much of the sting of death is removed as we talk about the love of Jesus Christ and the glories of heaven. Gently, compassionately, help the grieving parents to refocus their thinking from their loss to what we know to be their child's gain.

Prayer. Fourth, be bold in praying for and with your grieving friends. Take their sorrow to the Lord. Ask Him to heal their hearts, renew their strength, and fill them with the love and comfort of the Holy Spirit.

Encouragement. And finally, encourage the steps your grieving friends or loved ones take in reaching out to others in need. Thank them for sharing what the Lord has taught them through their experience. Give them a listening ear as they share with you their testimony. Allow them to share their story as fully as they desire—in many ways, they may be rehearsing with you what will become a truly evangelistic or edifying message to someone in deep distress in the not-too-distant future. Encourage their efforts at getting involved with others who are in need or who are going through a time of crisis. It is as they reach out to others that much of their healing will occur and they will find renewed purpose in their lives.

Do not be reluctant to get involved with a person who has lost a child, even if you yourself have not had this experience.

A listening ear, a loving heart, and warm expressions of acceptance and comfort are *always* welcome in time of loss. Even if you only say, "I'm sorry and I love you"—you will have said a great deal.

God calls us to minister His presence to one another, and there is no greater time for this ministry than when a parent has lost a child. If you have lost a child, allow others to minister to you. If you know of someone who has lost a child, reach out to that person with the love of the Lord. Trust God to show you what He would have you say, do, and pray.

NINE

Let Me Pray with You

IF YOU ARE A GRIEVING PARENT TODAY, I INVITE YOU TO pray this prayer with me:

Father, thank You for Your Word—the length and breadth and height of it that covers all issues of life. Thank You, Father, for the confidence You give us in Your Word about the eternal destiny of our little ones who die.

I thank You, Lord, for the little life who never saw the dawn of his or her birthday. I thank You for those who have lived for hours, days, months, or even years and then have been snatched away to heaven. I thank You for all the children who have passed through this world without ever knowing the taint or burden of sin, unbelief, or evil deeds.

Thank You for Your compassion on sinners. Thank You for saving this little one who had no ability to repent of his sin nature or believe in Christ Jesus. Thank You for receiving this little one in Your mercy.

For Your great grace and rescue of this little one, we truly give You our thanks and praise.

Heal the hearts of these parents, Lord, as they mourn the loss of their little one. Turn their sorrow to joy as they accept the truth that their little one is safely in Your arms—now and forevermore. Give them a renewed awareness of Your great plan and purpose for every life You have allowed to be conceived. Give them a renewed hope of heaven and a renewed reliance upon Your Word and Your presence with us at all times, in all situations, and even now in their sorrow.

We desire, Father, that You would help these parents to raise other children they may have now or in the future in the nurture and admonition of the Lord. Give these parents strength and wisdom to reach out to other children beyond their home, so they might fully understand the issues of law and grace, sin and salvation, and come to embrace Your Son, Jesus, as Savior and then follow Him as Lord.

In Christ's name we pray. Amen.

Notes

Chapter 2: What Can We Say with Certainty to Those with Empty Arms?

1. J. Cullberg, "Mental Reactions of Women to Perinatal Death" from *Psychosomatic Medicine in Obstetrics and Gynecology,* ed. N. Morris (Basel, Germany: S. Karger, 1971).

Chapter 3: How Does God Regard Children?

1. "Letter IX" from *The Works of John Newton* (London: Hamilton Adams, 1820), 182.

2. John Calvin, *Commentary on a Harmony of the Evangelists, Matthew, Mark, and Luke,* vol. 1 (Grand Rapids, Mich.: Baker Book House, 1981), 389–91.

Chapter 4: What If My Child Is Not Among the Elect?

1. Charles Spurgeon, "Expositions of the Doctrines of Grace," from *The Metropolitan Tabernacle Pulpit*, vol. 7 (London: Passmore and Alabaster, 1862), 300.

2. Loraine Boettner, *The Reformed Doctrine of Predestination* (Phillipsburg, N.J.: Presbyterian and Reformed Publishing Co., 1992), 142.

3. R. A. Webb, *The Theology of Infant Salvation* (Richmond, Va.: Presbyterian Committee of Publications, 1907), 42.

4. Phil Johnson, "What About Infants Who Die?" from unpublished sermon notes, 1999 (emphasis added).

Chapter 6: What Is My Child's Life Like in Heaven?

1. A. A. Hodge, *Evangelical Theology* (Carlisle, Pa.: Banner of Truth, 1976), 400.

About the Author

John MacArthur is pastor-teacher of Grace Community Church in Sun Valley, California, president of The Master's College and Seminary, and featured teacher with the Grace to You media ministry. The author of numerous bestselling books, MacArthur's popular expository style of teaching can be heard daily on the internationally syndicated radio broadcast *Grace to You*. He is also the author and general editor of *The MacArthur Study Bible*, which won a Gold Medallion award and has sold more than 500,000 copies. John and his wife, Patricia, have four grown children and twelve grandchildren.

For More Information

Grace to You is the Bible-teaching media ministry of John MacArthur. In addition to producing the worldwide *Grace to You* and *Grace to You Weekend* radio broadcasts, the ministry distributes books by John MacArthur and has produced more than thirteen million audiocassette lessons since 1969. For more details about John MacArthur and all his Bible-teaching resources, contact Grace to You at 800-55-GRACE or www.gty.org.

Also from John MacArthur

Can God Bless America? Dr. MacArthur, while pointing out that the Old Testament speaks of God's conditional blessings, asks the question most Americans choose to ignore: "Should God bless America?" This book calls the U.S. to turn back to God and shows how it can become a nation that is once again blessed by God.

ISBN 0-8499-5559-9;
Cassette ISBN 0-8499-6351-6

Unleashing God's Word in Your Life. You can learn to effectively apply Bible teachings and principles to your own life. This practical Bible study companion cuts to the heart of God's Word and shows you how to do the same.

ISBN 0-7852-5033-6

Terrorism, Jihad, and the Bible. September 11, 2001, saw the deadliest attack ever launched on American soil, leaving us asking questions such as, Why does God permit such things to happen? Dr. MacArthur points us to the Bible for answers to this and many other questions arising out of recent atrocities.

ISBN 0-8499-4367-1;
Spanish ISBN 0-8811-3719-7

Why One Way? A concise guide to understanding how and why the ancient Christian faith makes sense for today and a blueprint for communicating truth to a "truthless" and cynical generation.

ISBN 0-8499-5558-0

The MacArthur Study Bible. From the moment you pick it up, you'll know it is a classic. Winner of "The 1998 Study Bible of the Year Award" and featuring the word-for-word accuracy of the New King James Version, it is perfect for serious Bible study. (Since this Bible comes in a variety of styles, visit your bookstore to find the one that's right for you.)

Twelve Ordinary Men. Jesus chose ordinary men—fishermen, tax collectors, political zealots—and turned their weakness into strength, producing greatness from utter uselessness. MacArthur draws principles from Christ's careful, hands-on training of the original twelve disciples for today's modern disciple—you.

ISBN 0-8499-1773-5;
cassette ISBN 0-8499-6350-8;
workbook ISBN 0-8499-4407-4

Lord, Teach Me to Pray. Along with examples of prayer from Dr. MacArthur's own prayer life, this gift book includes classic Puritan prayers and pages to record personal prayers as well as God's answers. Teaching us how to pray, what to pray, and the purpose of prayer, it will deepen your fellowship with the Father.

ISBN 1-4041-0024-5

MacArthur LifeWorks Library CD-ROM. The interactivity and ease-of-use of *eBible*™ combined with the wealth of material available from John MacArthur provide a powerful electronic library!

ISBN 0-7852-5018-2

Hard to Believe—available November 2003. In contrast to the superficiality of much modern Christian teaching, Dr. John MacArthur serves up the unvarnished truth of what Christ taught and lived. In simple, compelling terms, MacArthur spells out what is required of those who would follow Him.

ISBN 0-7852-6345-4;
cassette ISBN 0-7852-6347-0;
CD ISBN 0-7852-6152-4

If this book has ministered to
you, please visit our Web site at
SafeInTheArmsOfGod.org
and leave a personal testimony,
a tribute to your child, or a note of
encouragement to other parents.